Oregon Bucket List Adventure Guide

Explore 100 Offbeat Destinations You Must Visit!

Sarah Gardner

Canyon Press
canyon@purplelink.org

Please consider writing a review!
Just visit: purplelink.org/review

ISBN: 978-1-957590-16-5

FREE BONUS

Discover 31 Incredible Places You Can
Visit Next! Just Go To:

purplelink.org/travel

Table of Contents

How to Use This Book

Welcome to your very own adventure guide to exploring the many wonders of the state of Oregon. Not only does this book offer the most wonderful places to visit and sights to see in the vast state, but it provides GPS coordinates for Google Maps to make exploring that much easier.

Adventure Guide
Sorted by region, this guide offers over 100 amazing wonders found in Oregon for you to see and explore. They can be visited in any order and this book will help you keep track of where you've been and where to look forward to going next. Each section describes the area or place, what to look for, how to get there, and what you may need to bring along.

GPS Coordinates
As you can imagine, not all of the locations in this book have a physical address. Fortunately, some of our listed wonders are either located within a National Park or Reserve, or near a city, town, or place of business. For those that are not associated with a specific location, it is easiest to map it using GPS coordinates.

Luckily, Google has a system of codes that converts the coordinates into pin-drop locations that Google Maps can interpret and navigate.

Each adventure in this guide includes GPS coordinates along with a physical address whenever it is available.

It is important that you are prepared for poor cell signals. It is recommended that you route your location and ensure that the directions are accessible offline. Depending on your device and the distance of some locations, you may need to travel with a backup battery source.

About Oregon

The Oregon Trail might be first to come to mind when thinking about this part of the Pacific Northwest, but the first European traders and settlers to explore what is now Oregon landed in the mid-1500s. These were mostly Spanish sailors sent northeast from the Philippines across the Pacific Ocean, and many of their ships wrecked on the Oregon Coast. As more settlers arrived, indigenous tribes who called the land home met similar fates as they did in other parts of the country; they were forcibly relocated to reservations, especially when Oregon became a U.S. territory in 1848.

Today, Oregon is known for large cities like Portland. These cities are famous for their thriving music scene as well as their food and drink. In fact, Portland has the largest number of breweries of any city in the world. Tourism makes up a large portion of the state's income, and while Portland is often a center for visitors, Oregon's many natural wonders draw climbers, hikers, rafters, kayakers, and nature enthusiasts from all over the world. Its often-remote natural beauty also attracts filmmakers; movies filmed in Oregon include *The Goonies*, *One Flew Over the Cuckoo's Nest*, and *Stand By Me*.

Landscape and Climate

Oregon is bordered by the Columbia River on its north side, which separates it from Washington State, as well as the Snake River on its east side, which separates it from Idaho. Oregon's landscape and climate have been affected by volcanic activity, which has formed canyons, lava flows, and even dry deserts.

The Oregon Coast stretches for 362 miles along the western edge, bordered by the vast Pacific Ocean and the Oregon Coast Mountain Range. The Oregon Coast National Wildlife Refuge Complex covers 320 of the 362 miles and protects the various species that call the coast home. The Oregon Coast has some of the most diverse marine ecology in the world. Several species of seals make their home there, and gray whales, humpback whales, and orcas migrate past Oregon every year on their way to the Arctic. Birders also prize this part of Oregon for its seabirds, shorebirds, and even birds of prey like bald eagles and ospreys.

The Oregon High Desert is located east of the Cascade Mountain Range and south of the Blue Mountains. Technically, much of the High Desert only qualifies as scrubland or steppe, but it still only averages approximately 0.6 inches of rainfall per year. Steens Mountain is the highest point at 9,733 feet above sea level, but the High Desert averages about 4,000 feet, giving the region its name. The vegetation that grows in the desert includes many of Oregon's native wildflowers, and the High Desert contains the oldest known tree in Oregon, a juniper tree that is estimated to be 1,600 years old. Hundreds of animal species can be found in the High Desert, from small mammals to birds of prey to bighorn sheep.

Oregon's forests might be the first on your mind when considering the state's natural beauty, but they're a little more spread out than the coast and desert. Densely forested areas concentrate in Willamette Valley, which contains the big cities of Portland and Salem, and the Columbia Plateau in northern Oregon. These temperate rain forests contain bigleaf maples, Douglas fir, and western hemlock. They also have some of the oldest and tallest trees in the Pacific Northwest in addition to several beautiful waterfalls.

Leslie Gulch

One of Oregon's most beautiful canyons, the Leslie Gulch is one of the popular ending spots for a trip down the Owyhee River. It also features some of the state's most beautiful rock formations and over 80 established climbing routes. You can hike one of the trails into Juniper Gulch or Timber Gulch or camp at the local Slocum Creek Campground.

Best Time to Visit: Flash floods can make the road into Leslie Gulch impassable, and with no cell service or Wi-Fi to call for help, it is best to visit in the summer.

Passes/Permits/Fees: There is no fee to visit.

Closest City or Town: Adrian

Physical Address:
Jordan Valley Chamber of Commerce
306 Blackaby Street
Jordan Valley, OR 97910

GPS Coordinates: 43.3118° N, 117.3153° W

Did You Know? The gulch was originally called Dugout, but it was renamed for Hiram Leslie, a local rancher who was struck by lightning in the canyon in 1882.

Astoria-Megler Bridge

Spanning the Columbia River, the 14-mile Astoria-Megler Bridge is the longest continuous truss bridge in North America. Before the bridge was in place, the only way to travel between Astoria, Oregon and the Washington side of the Columbia River was by ferry. Ferry service began in 1926 and operated through 1946, but because it didn't operate during bad weather, it was determined that a ferry was not a feasible transportation solution. Construction on the bridge began in November 1962, and it was completed in 1966.

Best Time to Visit: If you want to walk across the bridge, the best time to visit is during the Great Columbia Crossing, which occurs annually in October.

Passes/Permits/Fees: There is no fee.

Closest City or Town: Astoria

Physical Address:
Astoria Warrenton Area Chamber of Commerce
111 W. Marine Drive
Astoria, OR 97103

GPS Coordinates: 46.21648° N, 123.86225° W

Did You Know? There is only one day a year visitors can walk across the bridge!

Captain George Flavel House Museum

Once the home of Captain George Flavel—a Columbia River bar pilot and real estate investor—and his family, the Captain George Flavel House Museum is one of the best-preserved examples in the Northwest of Queen Anne–style architecture. The house has been restored to resemble what it would have looked like in the Victorian period and features historical artifacts. The residence, which was built in 1886, remained in the Flavel family until 1934, when it was gifted to Astoria.

Best Time to Visit: The Captain George Flavel House Museum is open daily from 10:00 a.m. to 5:00 p.m. during the period of May through September and 11:00 a.m. to 4:00 p.m. from October through April.

Passes/Permits/Fees: The museum costs $7 for adults, $6 for seniors, and $2 for children.

Closest City or Town: Astoria

Physical Address:
714 Exchange Street
Astoria, OR 97103

GPS Coordinates: 46.18859° N, 123.83575° W

Did You Know? The house was built overlooking the river, so that the captain could monitor local ship traffic.

Columbia River Maritime Museum

This museum was founded in 1962 by a group of naval veterans and fishing industry businessmen who wanted to preserve the maritime history of the Pacific Northwest. The Columbia River has long been a defining feature that shaped industries, formed the culture, and provided necessary resources to residents of and visitors to the region. The Columbia River Maritime Museum boasts more than 30,000 objects; over 20,000 photographs; and a 10,000-volume research library.

Best Time to Visit: The Columbia River Maritime Museum is open daily from 9:30 a.m. to 5:00 p.m.

Passes/Permits/Fees: The fee to visit the Columbia River Maritime Museum is $16 for adults, $13 for seniors ages 65 and older, and $5 for children between the ages of 6 and 17. Children ages 5 and under are free.

Closest City or Town: Astoria

Physical Address:
1792 Marine Drive
Astoria, OR 97103

GPS Coordinates: 46.19056° N, 123.82369° W

Did You Know? At one point, the Columbia River was a main thoroughfare for native trade routes.

Oregon Film Museum

Oregon has been the location for numerous films, many of which are embedded in American culture. The Oregon Film Museum celebrates this legacy through exhibits that allow visitors to recreate famous scenes. The Oregon Film Museum is located in the former Clatsop County Jail, which was in operation between 1914 and 1976. It was the working set for portions of *The Goonies*, *Short Circuit*, and *Come See the Paradise*.

Best Time to Visit: The museum is open daily October through April from 11:00 a.m. to 5:00 p.m. and May through September from 10:00 a.m. to 5:00 p.m.

Passes/Permits/Fees: The fee to visit the Oregon Film Museum is $6 for adults and $2 for children.

Closest City or Town: Astoria

Physical Address:
732 Duane Street
Astoria, OR 97103

GPS Coordinates: 46.18937° N, 123.83530 W

Did You Know? The first film set in Oregon and Astoria was *The Fisherman's Bride* in 1909.

The Astoria Column

In 1898, a dream was conceived to build an electrified tower in Astoria that would rivel Gustav Eiffel's tower in Paris, France. Coxcomb Hill was selected for the site of this tower because of its stunning panoramic views of the Oregon landscape. In 1911, when Astoria celebrated its centennial, public interest in such a tower grew, and fundraising efforts to build the tower began in earnest. A 525-foot-long engraved mural that acts as a histogram commemorating events in the Pacific Northwest's history wraps around the column, a design that was applied by Italian artist Attilio Pusterla using the *sgraffito* technique.

Best Time to Visit: Visit at night to view the light show.

Passes/Permits/Fees: There is a $5 parking fee.

Closest City or Town: Astoria

Physical Address:
1 Coxcomb Drive
Astoria, OR 97103

GPS Coordinates: 46.18191° N, 123.81756° W

Did You Know? There are 164 steps on a spiral staircase that allow visitors to climb to the observation deck of the Astoria Column.

National Historic Oregon Trail Interpretive Center

The National Historic Oregon Trail Interpretive Center uses life-size displays, live theater presentations, films, and other living history demonstrations, exhibits, and special events to tell the story of explorers, pioneers, and settlers who traveled the Oregon Trail to tame the frontier west. Encompassing 500 acres, visitors can see the remains of the Flagstaff Gold Mine, ruts in the road that were carved by pioneer wagons, and over 4 miles of interpretive trails.

Best Time to Visit: Visit in spring, summer, or fall for more comfortable weather.

Passes/Permits/Fees: There is no fee to visit.

Closest City or Town: Baker City

Physical Address:
22267 OR-86
Baker City, OR 97814

GPS Coordinates: 44.81571° N, 117.72867° W

Did You Know? The National Historic Oregon Trail Interpretive Center is located on Flagstaff Hill, which provided pioneers with their first look of the Blue Mountains, signaling the end of their arduous journey.

Arnold Ice Cave

Arnold Ice Cave is yet another testament to Oregon's volcanic history. The cave is actually part of a system created by a lava flow. The lava tubes are around 80,000 years old, but Arnold Ice Cave was not discovered by Americans until 1889. Unfortunately, due to vandalism and defacement by climbers, there are large sections of the cave system that are closed for restoration. Take the Hidden Forest and Arnold Ice Cave Trail down to the cave's entrance. This hike falls short of 1 mile and is good for all skill levels. Temperatures in the cave hover just above freezing, so dress warmly.

Best Time to Visit: Arnold Ice Cave is closed from November to April to protect the hibernation of bats.

Passes/Permits/Fees: There is no fee to visit.

Closest City or Town: Bend

Physical Address:
Visit Bend
750 NW Lava Road, #160
Bend, OR 97703

GPS Coordinates: 43.95158° N, 121.25062° W

Did You Know? The cave was once used to excavate ice before electricity was available.

Bend Ale Trail

The Bend Ale Trail is a tour of more than 24 breweries in Bend Oregon. It began in 2010 with just six breweries and has grown significantly due to the area's renowned craft beer brewers. The breweries are spread across seven territories. The Old Block is the epicenter of the craft beer scene; The Western Front features laid-back breweries with sunny patios; The Riverlands line the banks of the Deschutes River; The Badlands is considered adventurous; The Brewer's District features craft beer direct from the source; The Far North is a friendly territory providing frontier hospitality; and The Outer Rim is filled with new discoveries.

Best Time to Visit: Any time of year.

Passes/Permits/Fees: There is no fee to visit.

Closest City or Town: Bend

Physical Address:
Visit Bend
750 NW Lava Road, Suite 160
Bend, OR 97703

GPS Coordinates: 44.05868° N, 121.31135° W

Did You Know? A keepsake passport can be purchased at the visitor's center for $5 to record your adventure.

Big Obsidian Flow

This lava flow located in the Newberry Caldera looks nearly identical to when it first cooled after erupting from a magma chamber. A trail with several interpretive signs details the history and geology of the flow. The trail is a loop that extends a bit longer than half a mile. It's mostly flat and easy, but it's important to be extremely careful since the trail is surrounded by volcanic glass. Wear closed-toed shoes, stay on the trail, and take it easy. If you're looking to sit and learn, rangers give talks about Oregon's volcanic history and the national monument throughout the summer.

Best Time to Visit: The best time to visit Big Obsidian Flow is between June and October.

Passes/Permits/Fees: There is a $5 parking fee.

Closest City or Town: Bend

Physical Address:
Deschutes National Forest
63095 Deschutes Market Road
Bend, OR 97701

GPS Coordinates: 43.6957° N, 121.2345° W

Did You Know? At a mere 1,300 years old, the Big Obsidian lava flow is actually the youngest in Oregon.

Cascade Lakes Scenic Byway

Beginning as Century Drive at the "Flaming Chicken" roundabout at 14th Street and Galveston Avenue, the Cascade Lakes Scenic Byway is a 66-mile drive that can take up to 5 hours to complete if you decide to make all stops along the way. The road winds through the Deschutes National Forest, where there are two major waterfalls and a must-do hiking opportunity beside the Deschutes River. Stunning views of Mt. Bachelor, Broken Top, and the Three Sisters are only part of the reason you'll love this drive.

Best Time to Visit: The road may close during the winter, so visit during the spring, summer, or fall.

Passes/Permits/Fees: There is a $5 day-use fee to visit the Deschutes National Forest and drive the byway.

Closest City or Town: Bend

Physical Address:
Visit Bend
750 NW Lava Road, #160
Bend, OR 97703

GPS Coordinates: 44.03449° N, 121.33814° W

Did You Know? The byway passes through a region of Oregon that gets 250 sunny days each year.

Crux Fermentation Project

The Crux Fermentation Project is a craft beer brewery committed to fermentative experimentation to produce some of the highest-quality beer in the country. Throughout the years, Crux Fermentation Project has tried everything from rare yeast strains and whole leaf hops to nontraditional brewing methods and experimental aging processes to find new beer blends and styles.

Best Time to Visit: The tasting room at Crux Fermentation Project is open Wednesday through Monday from 11:30 a.m. to 9:00 p.m. and on Tuesday from 3:00 p.m. to 9:00 p.m.

Passes/Permits/Fees: There is no fee to visit Crux Fermentation Project, but there is a cost to taste beer.

Closest City or Town: Bend

Physical Address:
50 SW Division Street
Bend, OR 97702

GPS Coordinates: 44.05155° N, 121.30799° W

Did You Know? They also fermented whiskey, wine, cider, pickles, and kraut!

Deschutes Brewery

The Deschutes Brewery originally opened as a small brewpub in 1988. It was designed to be a community gathering place and was initially named The Deschutes Brewery & Public House. Since then, the brewpub has expanded to include a brewery and tasting room located on the banks of its namesake, the Deschutes River. The owners believe that "everyone is equal over a beer," and supports various nonprofits that focus on diversity and inclusion, water and land conservation, youth services, and hunger prevention.

Best Time to Visit: The Deschutes Brewery is open daily from 11:30 a.m. to 9:00 p.m.

Passes/Permits/Fees: There is no fee to visit the Deschutes Brewery, but there is a cost for the beers.

Closest City or Town: Bend

Physical Address:
1044 NW Bond Street
Bend, OR 97703

GPS Coordinates: 44.06029° N, 121.31113° W

Did You Know? The Deschutes Brewery sells over 225,000 barrels of craft beer each year.

High Desert Museum

Established in 1982, the High Desert Museum offers 135 acres and 100,000 square feet of exhibit space to tell the story of early Oregon explorers and settlers. Visitors can explore an authentic sawmill and homestead built in 1904 and learn about Native American Culture through interactive programs.

Best Time to Visit: Visit the museum April 1 through October 31 from 9:00 a.m. to 5:00 p.m. and November 1 through March 31 from 10:00 a.m. to 4:00 p.m.

Passes/Permits/Fees: Between April 1 and October 31, the costs $17 for adults, $14 for college students or seniors ages 65 and older, and $10 for children ages 3 to 12. Between November 1 and March 31, fees are $14 for adults, $12 for students or seniors, and $9 for children.

Closest City or Town: Bend

Physical Address:
59800 US-97
Bend, OR 97702

GPS Coordinates: 43.96704° N, 121.34149° W

Did You Know? The High Desert Museum boasts a collection of about 29,000 objects from the Pacific Northwest, Great Basin, and Plateau territories.

Lava River Cave

Lava River Cave is part of the Newberry National Volcanic Monument, and its northwest passage is the longest continuous lava tube in Oregon at 5,211 feet. The cave was formed in a volcanic eruption nearly 80,000 years ago when newer layers of lava crusted over the top of the lava river, sealing it inside. Exploring the cave takes 1.5 hours. Two light sources are recommended, and the path alternates between stairways, flat boardwalk, and uneven surfaces.

Best Time to Visit: The Lava River Cave is open from May to September and closed in the winter.

Passes/Permits/Fees: There is a $5 day-pass fee to visit the cave. Light sources can be rented for $5.

Closest City or Town: Bend

Physical Address:
Deschutes National Forest
63095 Deschutes Market Road
Bend, OR 97701

GPS Coordinates: 43.8955° N, 121.3697° W

Did You Know? Exploring the last 310 feet of the cave requires crawling on your hands and knees and takes at least 30 minutes.

Mt. Bachelor

Mt. Bachelor is located at the northern end of the 15-mile-long Mount Bachelor Volcanic Chain. This chain underwent four major volcanic eruptions during the Pleistocene and Holocene eras, but it is not considered a threat of becoming an active volcano at any time in the near future. Skiing is a favorite activity at the Mount Bachelor Ski Area, which originally opened in 1958 and is currently one of the largest ski areas in the Pacific Northwest. It features a skiable area of over 3,600 acres and a vertical drop of more than 3,300 feet. There are also many other activities to enjoy on the mountain!

Best Time to Visit: There are activities year-round!

Passes/Permits/Fees: An all-mountain lift ticket at Mount Bachelor Ski Area is $65 per person.

Closest City or Town: Bend

Physical Address:
Mount Bachelor Ski Area
13000 SW Century Drive
Bend, OR 97702

GPS Coordinates: 43.98200° N, 121.68930° W

Did You Know? Mt. Bachelor got its name from its position apart from the nearby Three Sisters mountains.

No Name Lake

This "lake without a name," located amid the snowy peaks of the Cascade Mountain Range, is one of Oregon's best-kept secrets. During spring and summer, the pure turquoise waters overlook an excellent view of Broken Top Mountain, the Three Sisters, and Oregon's valleys and forests. The lake is only accessible on foot and the hike itself is around 15 miles and offers very little cover from the Oregon sun. The last stretch requires you to scramble up a very steep creek bed. It is important to bring plenty of fluids and make sure you are prepared.

Best Time to Visit: Due to its elevation, this area is generally only open from April to October.

Passes/Permits/Fees: There is a $5 parking fee.

Closest City or Town: Bend

Physical Address:
Visit Bend
750 NW Lava Road, #160
Bend, OR 97703

GPS Coordinates: 44.0809° N, 121.6871° W

Did You Know? No Name Lake is a glacial lake and receives its deep turquoise color from the Crook Glacier.

Old Mill District

The Old Mill District is a popular shopping and entertainment area located along the Deschutes River. It is home to independent shops, upscale chain stores, tasting rooms, restaurants, riverside trails, and the Hayden Homes Amphitheater, Oregon's largest outdoor concert venue. The amphitheater hosts over a dozen concerts in the summer. In addition to the relatively new restaurants and shops in the district, visitors can explore nine historically renovated buildings.

Best Time to Visit: Each shop and restaurant has its own operating hours. Check the website for details.

Passes/Permits/Fees: There is no fee to visit the Old Mill District but be sure to bring money for shopping.

Closest City or Town: Bend

Physical Address:
450 SW Powerhouse Drive
Bend, OR 97702

GPS Coordinates: 44.04707° N, 121.31500° W

Did You Know? The architecture is inspired by the Brooks-Scanlon lumber mill that was a primary economic driver for Bend for most of the 20th century.

Oregon High Desert

The majority of the region surrounding the Oregon High Desert is classified as steppe or scrubland rather than actual desert. While recreation is allowed in the high desert, its primary use is for agricultural purposes, with livestock ranches and private grazing land dotting the area. There are several rivers that flow through the desert, providing many opportunities for recreation.

Best Time to Visit: The best time to visit the Oregon High Desert is in the fall when the high temperatures are in the 70s, the leaves are changing colors, and tens of thousands of birds are migrating through the area.

Passes/Permits/Fees: There is no fee to visit.

Closest City or Town: Bend

Physical Address:
Visit Bend
750 NW Lava Road, #160
Bend, OR 97703

GPS Coordinates: 43.66854° N, 120.33456° W

Did You Know? The Northern Paiute tribe is the name for the Indigenous people who lived in the high-desert region.

South Sister

The geologically youngest and tallest mountain of the Three Sisters, the South Sister is the third-tallest mountain in Oregon and home to the highest lake in the state. It is also the sister that has experienced the most recent volcanic activity, having demonstrated lava activity approximately 2,000 years ago. The south-side route to the summit is popular in the summer, as it can be climbed with minimal technical skill or equipment. The ascent begins from either Devils Lake or Green Lakes and follows a well-worn trail.

Best Time to Visit: The best time to climb the South Sister is in the summer.

Passes/Permits/Fees: There is a $5 fee per vehicle.

Closest City or Town: Bend

How to get there:
Deschutes National Forest
53095 Deschutes Market Road
Bend, OR 97701

GPS Coordinates: 44.09226° N, 121.77813° W

Did You Know? There is a growing bulge on the west side of the South Sister, indicating that magma may be moving below the mountain's surface.

Tumalo Falls

Tumalo Falls may seem little with a 97-foot drop, but this popular waterfall has plenty of merits. With an area for picnicking and several trails for hiking and mountain biking, there's a lot to do in this section of Deschutes National Forest. The hike is moderate and features a few add-ons if you're craving a longer jaunt, but the hike to the waterfall viewing platform is only a quarter mile. Hiking another 1.25 miles leads to Middle Tumalo Falls, a 65-foot, two-tiered cascade.

Best Time to Visit: The trail to Tumalo Falls can be hiked year-round, but the access road closes in the winter. Visit at the end of spring for a beautiful sight.

Passes/Permits/Fees: There is a $5 parking fee.

Closest City or Town: Bend

Physical Address:
Deschutes National Forest
63095 Deschutes Market Road
Bend, OR 97701

GPS Coordinates: 44.0340° N, 121.5669° W

Did You Know? Tumalo Creek is 20 miles long and provides water for farmland and drinking for the city of Bend.

Terwilliger Hot Springs

These pristine geothermal pools are natural hot springs, accessed by a quarter-mile trail from the parking lot through the forest, where you are shielded by a canopy of treetops and offered a view of a beautiful lagoon and Rider Creek Falls. The six pools are clothing optional and range in temperature from 85 to 112°F. The area is day-use only and alcohol is not permitted.

Best Time to Visit: The road to the parking lot for Terwilliger Hot Springs is not maintained for snow and ice, so it's best to hit this one before it starts to snow in late autumn.

Passes/Permits/Fees: There is a $7 fee for access to the Terwilliger Hot Springs area.

Closest City or Town: Blue River

Physical Address:
Willamette National Forest
3106 Pierce Parkway
Springfield, OR 97477

GPS Coordinates: 44.0830° N, 122.2384° W

Did You Know? The Terwilliger Hot Springs is also known as the Cougar Hot Springs since the springs drain into the Cougar Reservoir.

Boardman Tree Farm

The 25,000-acre Boardman Tree Farm features thousands of hybrid poplar trees, all neatly arranged in evenly spaced rows. The farm is sectioned into 40-acre and 70-acre plots intersected by roads. There are about 600 trees per acre. When the trees reach maturity they are cut down and sent to a sawmill to be made into boards and wood chips. The wood chips are then made into paper, and any trees that can't be turned into lumber or paper are converted to hog fuel or pulp. Everything at the farm is used for other purposes. Tours of the meticulously planned farm are available for free but require reservations.

Best Time to Visit: It is best to visit during the fall.

Passes/Permits/Fees: There is no fee to visit.

Closest City or Town: Boardman

Physical Address:
73669 Homestead Lane
Boardman, OR 97818

GPS Coordinates: 45.81858° N, 119.53697° W

Did You Know? To properly water the trees, nine 1,000-horsepower pumps draw in water from the Columbia River at 117,000 gallons per minute.

Natural Bridges Cove

This hidden gem is something straight out of a fairytale! Giant sea arches rise out of the swirling, turquoise water as it enters and exits the cove. The trail down to the scenic viewing platform features quick elevation gain at the end, but it is well marked and easy to follow. Once you reach the viewpoint, you're treated with an incredible view. It is possible to reach the natural bridges yourself, but it is dangerous to do so and very easy to slip and fall.

Best Time to Visit: Visit Natural Bridges Cove at sunrise or sunset for the best photography lighting. Stop by in spring for a hike through Oregon's wildflowers.

Passes/Permits/Fees: There is no fee to visit.

Closest City or Town: Brookings

Physical Address:
Brookings City Hall Visitor Center
898 Elk Drive
Brookings, OR 97415

GPS Coordinates: 42.94515° N, 124.45234° W

Did You Know? Natural Bridges Cove is part of the 20-mile Samuel H. Boardman State Scenic Corridor, which runs alongside Oregon's southern coast.

Samuel H. Boardman State Scenic Corridor

The 12-mile Samuel H. Boardman State Scenic Corridor winds past secluded beaches, offshore rock formations, and steep vertical bluffs as it traces the ocean shoreline. Located between Gold Beach and Brookings, this stretch of highway provides numerous opportunities. For photo-worthy sunsets and whale watching in the spring and fall, stop at Cape Ferrelo Viewpoint. To access side trails to several secluded beaches, visit House Rock Viewpoint.

Best Time to Visit: The best time to visit the is in the spring or fall to see whales migrating south.

Passes/Permits/Fees: It is free to visit.

Closest City or Town: Brookings

Physical Address:
Brookings City Hall Visitor Center
898 Elk Drive
Brookings, OR 97415

GPS Coordinates: 42.09112° N, 124.33023° W

Did You Know? To see the seven iconic arch rocks and a memorial to Dr. Samuel Dicken, be sure not to miss the Natural Bridge.

Crystal Crane Hot Springs

This small, family-owned business has been hosting tourists at its natural hot springs for more than 90 years. Guests can enjoy a soak in the cedar-enclosed bathhouse, in a public pond, or from a private pool included with their accommodations. The springs were discovered in 1920 and recognized as an excellent location for a resort that offered an alternative type of accommodations for travelers. The Crane Creek Inn, the sheepherders wagon, and some of the on-site teepees feature private soaking tubs.

Best Time to Visit: Crystal Crane Host Springs is open daily from 7:00 a.m. to 10:00 p.m. for day use.

Passes/Permits/Fees: The day-use fee to visit Crystal Crane Hot Springs is $5 per person for 4 hours. Rates vary for overnight stays.

Closest City or Town: Burns

Physical Address:
59315 OR-78
Burns, OR 97720

GPS Coordinates: 43.44192° N, 118.63887° W

Did You Know? The Hot Springs Pond holds about 323,143 gallons of fresh mineral water.

Cannon Beach

This popular tourist destination is a favorite destination for both locals and tourists because of its proximity to Portland. The beach hosts an annual sand castle-building contest in June and a parade on Independence Day. On the first Sunday in May, galleries host Spring Unveiling, an annual arts festival. There is also the Stormy Weather Arts Festival in the late fall. At the end of this event, an auction allows visitors to bid on and purchase select artwork from the festival.

Best Time to Visit: The best time to visit Cannon Beach is during the spring, summer, or fall for festivals.

Passes/Permits/Fees: There is no fee to visit.

Closest City or Town: Cannon Beach

Physical Address:
Cannon Beach Visitor Center
207 N. Spruce Street
Cannon Beach, OR 97110

GPS Coordinates: 45.89931° N, 123.95969° W

Did You Know? Within the city limits of Cannon Beach, there are four parks: Haystack Hill State Park, John Yeon State Natural Site, Tolovana Beach State Recreation Site, and Les Shirley Park.

Ecola State Park

Ecola State Park is 9 miles of coastline between Cannon Beach and Seaside Beach, wrapping around Tillamook Head. While hiking is the primary draw to this state park, surfing, tide-pooling, picnicking, and wildlife observation are other attractions that bring visitors to this waterfront park. The many hikes that originate here lead to cliffside views of hidden coves, forest-covered promontories, and even an abandoned lighthouse. There is an 8-mile hike that's a segment of the Oregon Coast Trail and a 2.5-mile historical hike called the Clatsop Loop Trail.

Best Time to Visit: The best time to visit Ecola State Park is in the summer due to mild weather.

Passes/Permits/Fees: There is a $5 fee per vehicle.

Closest City or Town: Cannon Beach

Physical Address:
207 N. Spruce Street
Cannon Beach, OR 97110

GPS Coordinates: 45.92077° N, 123.97399° W

Did You Know? Bald Point Site features a shell midden and house pit that date back to 1550 CE from the Tillamook Native American tribe.

Haystack Rock

Towering over visitors at a whopping 235 feet, Haystack Rock is a 15-million-year-old sea stack made of volcanic basalt. The rock was formed by lava flows from the Blue Mountains and was once attached to the coastline. It now stands separate due to the millions of years of erosion. Many different kinds of marine life can be viewed while visiting the rock, especially during summer at low tide when tidepools are full of interesting creatures.

Best Time to Visit: Haystack Rock can be seen at all times of the year, but if you're walking out to it, you should wait for low tide!

Passes/Permits/Fees: There is no fee to visit.

Closest City or Town: Cannon Beach

Physical Address:
Cannon Beach Chamber of Commerce
207 N. Spruce Street
Cannon Beach, OR 97110

GPS Coordinates: 45.8841° N, 123.9686° W

Did You Know? Haystack Rock can famously be seen in the background of the opening scene from *The Goonies* as the Fratellis flee the police.

Multnomah Falls

Multnomah Falls measures 620 feet, making it the tallest waterfall in Oregon. According to a legend from the local Multnomah tribe, the waterfall was formed after the self-sacrifice of a young woman who pleaded with the Great Spirit to save her village from plague; she jumped from the cliff, and the water began to flow from above. From the Multnomah Falls Visitor Center, follow the steep trail across Benson Bridge, which crosses about 105 feet over the lower cascade. If you're feeling adventurous, continue to follow the trail up to a small viewing area at the very top of the falls.

Best Time to Visit: To avoid crowds, aim for the fall or winter for an unforgettable view.

Passes/Permits/Fees: There is no fee to visit.

Closest City or Town: Cascade Locks

Physical Address:
Columbia River Gorge National Scenic Area
902 Wasco Avenue
Hood River, OR 97031

GPS Coordinates: 45.5762° N, 122.1158° W

Did You Know? Multnomah Falls is the most-visited natural site in the Pacific Northwest.

Out'n'About Treehouse Treesort

Looking for a unique alternative to traditional hotel rooms? Look no further than the Out'n'About Treehouse Treesort. This "resort" offers several luxury treehouses for adventurers who want to camp in the wooded area right next to the Siskiyou National Forest. This legal bed and breakfast not only offers the most interesting sleeping quarters you'll ever find, but it also provides numerous "activitrees," such as ziplining, horseback rides, and hiking adventures that originate right from the treesort.

Best Time to Visit: Summer is the peak season. So, visit in the winter for lower rates.

Passes/Permits/Fees: Rates start at $50 per night. Check the website for all pricing details.

Closest City or Town: Cave Junction

Physical Address:
300 Page Creek Road
Cave Junction, OR 97523

GPS Coordinates: 42.03798° N, 123.62340° W

Did You Know? The Majestree at the Out'n'About Treehouse Resort is the tallest treehouse at 47 feet from the ground.

Rogue Valley ZipLine Adventure

Rogue Valley ZipLine Adventure features five zipline courses throughout the historic gold-mining hills in southern Oregon. Enjoy a basic zipline tour that includes three hours of zipping across 2,700 feet with two certified zipline guides. Or, if you want to make a full day of it, book the Zip, Dip, & Sip Tour that includes the full Basic Zipline tour, lunch, rafting, and a wine tasting. On both tours, you'll pass through a replica 1800s gold-mining town.

Best Time to Visit: The Zip, Dip, & Sip Tour is only available seasonally, and reservations are required for all tours.

Passes/Permits/Fees: The fee to participate in the Basic Zipline tour is between $88 and $98 per person.

Closest City or Town: Central Point

Physical Address:
9450 Old Stage Road
Central Point, OR 97502

GPS Coordinates: 42.42179 N, 123.04115° W

Did You Know? You'll be treated to stunning views of Crater Lake Rim, Table Rocks, and Mount McLoughlin, among others.

Train Mountain Railroad

Founded in 1987 by Quentin Breen, the Train Mountain Railroad is the world's largest miniature railroad featuring more than 36 miles of 7.5-gauge track across 2,205 acres of pine forest. Breen himself assembled the property and developed more than 25 miles of track before passing away in 2008. The attraction is currently operated by Friends of Train Mountain.

Best Time to Visit: Visit on a Saturday between Memorial Day Weekend and Labor Day Weekend to have the opportunity to ride the Klamath & Western Railroad train between 10:00 a.m. and 3:00 p.m.

Passes/Permits/Fees: There is no fee to visit.

Closest City or Town: Chiloquin

Physical Address:
Train Mountain Railroad
36941 S. Chiloquin Road
Chiloquin, OR 97624

GPS Coordinates: 42.56043° N, 121.88691° W

Did You Know? The Train Mountain Railroad Museum features an exhibit of snow-fighting equipment that was used by the Southern Pacific and OC&E railroads in the Cascade Mountains to keep the tracks free of snow.

Crack in the Ground

The "crack" is actually an ancient volcanic fissure formed thousands of years ago when four volcanoes erupted, creating the Four Craters Lava Field, a shallow depression in the earth. The crack runs along the western edge for over 2 miles and is 70 feet deep. Hikers can explore the main fissure and the various crevices, caves, and formations that split off. It is a moderate hike, with some sandy and rocky areas and sharp lava rocks that can be dangerous. There are primitive campsites on Green Mountain near the fissure.

Best Time to Visit: The trail through the fissure is open year-round, but access might require a four-wheel-drive vehicle in the winter.

Passes/Permits/Fees: There is no fee.

Closest City or Town: Christmas Valley

Physical Address:
Christmas Valley Tourist Information
87217 Christmas Valley Highway
Christmas Valley, OR 97641

GPS Coordinates: 43.3336° N, 120.6723° W

Did You Know? The temperature in the fissure can be 20 to 30 degrees cooler than on the surface.

Fort Rock

About 100,000 years ago, basalt magma from beneath the Earth's surface pushed through what is now known as Fort Rock Lake and created a ring of tuff around half a mile in diameter. Over millennia, waves from the lake wore away at the ring until it was shaped into a jagged formation with straight sides. Fort Rock now looms up to 300 feet above a dry lakebed covered in sage and brush. It is also home to some of the oldest-known human artifacts in North America. Archaeologists have discovered a variety of woven sandals estimated between 9,000 and 13,000 years old.

Best Time to Visit: There is not much in terms of shade, so aim for a cloudy day.

Passes/Permits/Fees: There is no fee.

Closest City or Town: Christmas Valley

Physical Address:
Christmas Valley Tourist Information
87217 Christmas Valley Highway
Christmas Valley, OR 97641

GPS Coordinates: 43.3568° N, 121.0548° W

Did You Know? The community of Fort Rock, Oregon is one of two homestead-era communities that remain.

Waldo Lake

Waldo Lake is the second-deepest lake in Oregon with a maximum depth of 420 feet. Just like Crater Lake, the water at Waldo is so clear that you can see depths of up to 120 feet on a clear day. Conservationists have taken many steps to preserve the water purity of Waldo Lake, including banning gasoline-powered boats and limiting the top speed of boats with electric motors. Waldo Lake is a popular site for various water recreational activities, including swimming, canoeing, kayaking, and sailing.

Best Time to Visit: Visit in spring during the off-season.

Passes/Permits/Fees: Some trails and day-use activities may require a recreation pass. Current details are listed on the forest service's website.

Closest City or Town: Crescent Lake Junction

Physical Address:
Willamette National Forest
57600 McKenzie Highway
McKenzie Bridge, OR 97413

GPS Coordinates: 43.7270° N, 122.0445° W

Did You Know? The lake is named after John B. Waldo, an Oregon judge who advocated for land conservation.

Metolius Balancing Rocks

The location of the Balancing Rocks in Cove Palisades State Park was once a well-kept secret for park rangers only. In 2002, that changed when a wildfire decimated the overgrown juniper-pine forest that concealed the rocks. The peculiar Balancing Rocks offer a fascinating look into Oregon's volcanic history. The standing spires were created in one volcanic eruption, while the balanced rocks were created in subsequent eruptions. When erosion began, the rocks on top guarded their spires down below, protecting and preserving them. The trail to the rocks is an easy quarter mile trek.

Best Time to Visit: The rocks are visible year-round.

Passes/Permits/Fees: There is a $5 entrance fee.

Closest City or Town: Culver

Physical Address:
Oregon HooDoos Trailhead
Montgomery Rd
Culver, OR 97734

GPS Coordinates: 44.57850° N, 121.42178° W

Did You Know? The National Park Service feared that the formations would attract vandals, so the location was not publicized on any maps until after the fire.

Breitenbush Hot Springs

Breitenbush Hot Springs is the home of a worker-owned cooperative that exists on 154 acres of rugged mountain land. The workers, who also live there, serve thousands of people each year at the natural hot springs. The Breitenbush Hot Springs lodge was once part of a 1920s hot springs resort, and people would flock to the area to heal from illnesses thought to be helped by hot mineral water. The hot springs are now primarily used as a healing retreat and conference center.

Best Time to Visit: Breitenbush Hot Springs is open daily between 9:00 a.m. and 6:00 p.m.

Passes/Permits/Fees: There is a $35 fee for adults and a $20 fee for children ages 5 to 17 to visit Breitenbush Hot Springs. Children ages 4 and under are free.

Closest City or Town: Detroit

Physical Address:
53000 Breitenbush Road SE
Detroit, OR 97342

GPS Coordinates: 44.78205° N, 121.97549° W

Did You Know? Breitenbush Hot Springs are named for John Breitenbush, a one-armed hunter.

Mount Jefferson

This stratovolcano is the second-highest mountain in Oregon and considered one of the most difficult volcanoes to reach. Despite its ruggedness and remoteness, it is still a popular tourist destination. Mount Jefferson is named after the third U.S. president, Thomas Jefferson, who sponsored the Lewis and Clark Expedition that first saw the peak in 1806. Mount Jefferson hasn't erupted for at least 35,000 years and is unlikely to erupt in the near future. Visitors are unable to drive to Mount Jefferson, as there are no paved roads within 4 miles, and it is only accessible on foot or horse.

Best Time to Visit: Visit in spring, summer, or fall when the weather is mild.

Passes/Permits/Fees: Mount Jefferson is free to visit.

Closest City or Town: Detroit

Physical Address:
44125 N. Santiam Highway SE
Detroit, OR 97342

GPS Coordinates: 44.67744° N, 121.79954° W

Did You Know? Mount Jefferson is also known as Seekseekqua, the Native American name for the mountain.

Opal Creek

Opal Creek is a pristine stream surrounded by a gigantic forest of trees that range from 450 to 1,000 years old. It is one of the more remote wildernesses in Oregon. There are eight trails in the wilderness, ranging from 2 to 17 miles. For a moderate hike, try the Henline Falls trail with a 1.8-mile out-and-back climb. More experienced hikers may want to tackle the Little North Santiam Trail.

Best Time to Visit: The trailhead to Opal Creek is open all year, but this is a good hike for the summer.

Passes/Permits/Fees: There is a $5 day-use parking fee to visit Opal Creek. Check to see if any permits are applicable to you on the forest service website.

Closest City or Town: Detroit

Physical Address:
Detroit Ranger Station Visitor Center
44125 N. Santiam Highway
Detroit, OR 97360

GPS Coordinates: 44.859856° N, 122.264394° W

Did You Know? The Opal Creek Wilderness was threatened by the logging industry until 1998 when a wilderness bill protected it as a scenic recreation area.

The Dunes

Oregon's dunes tower up to 500 feet above sea level and stretch for 40 miles along the coast from North Bend to Florence. View the dunes from the Oregon Dunes Overlook just south of Dune City. There are also three main areas approved for off-highway vehicle use, and lots of rivers, lakes, and the Pacific Ocean for those interested in water sports.

Best Time to Visit: If you come between March and September, be sure to check which areas are protected for nesting snowy plovers!

Passes/Permits/Fees: There is a $5 day-use fee. Some activities may require a permit, and the current pricings are listed on the forest service's website.

Closest City or Town: Dune City

Physical Address:
Oregon Dunes National Recreation Area Visitor Center
855 US-101
Reedsport, OR 97467

GPS Coordinates: 43.7035° N, 124.1060° W

Did You Know? The famous science fiction setting of Arrakis in *Dune* by Frank Herbert was partly inspired by the Oregon dunes.

Bagby Hot Springs

Bagby Hot Springs are open for use 24 hours a day, making them unique and popular among the state's hot springs. There are three bathhouses on site, the main one featuring five cedar log tubs in five private rooms. The lower bathhouse includes three log tubs and a large round tub on an open deck. There is also a historic cabin and shed that can be explored during the day. The Shower Creek Campground is located just 0.25 miles from the trail to the springs. The campground is also the location of the Shower Falls trailhead that offers an easy, peaceful hike to a pretty waterfall.

Best Time to Visit: Visit during the spring or fall.

Passes/Permits/Fees: There is a $5 fee per person.

Closest City or Town: Estacada

Physical Address:
Mt. Hood National Forest
16400 Champion Way
Sandy, OR 97055

GPS Coordinates: 44.93880° N, 122.17435° W

Did You Know? Mike and Tamarah Rysavy, a couple who met at Bagby Hot Springs in 2001 and married, took over operations of the site in 2021.

Olallie Lake Resort

Founded in 1932, the ambiance of the Olallie Lake Resort has intentionally remained close to what it was in the 1930s and still includes a small general store, wood-burning stoves, kerosene lanterns, pit toilets, and outside water spigots. Popular activities at the resort include fishing and hiking the Pacific Crest Trail. The resort takes "rustic" to a whole new level, as there is no gas available nearby, internet service, cell phone service, no way to accept credit cards, and no ATM.

Best Time to Visit: The best time to visit is in the summer since the resort is closed in winter.

Passes/Permits/Fees: The fee to visit Olallie Lake Resort varies based on the accommodations and dates you select. See the website for pricing details.

Closest City or Town: Estacada

Physical Address:
Visit Estacada
475 SE Main Street
Estacada, OR 97023

GPS Coordinates: 44.81468° N, 121.78896° W

Did You Know? There are seven campgrounds in the Olallie Lake Resort area, all of which are primitive.

Jordan Schnitzer Museum of Art

Located on the campus of the University of Oregon in Eugene, the Jordan Schnitzer Museum of Art (originally named the University of Oregon Art Museum) has been open to the public since 1933. Initially, the museum was conceived and built to house the Murray Warner Collection of Oriental Art, of which 3,700 works were donated to the university by Gertrude Bass Warner.

Best Time to Visit: The museum is open Thursday through Sunday from 11:00 a.m. to 5:00 p.m. and on Wednesday from 11:00 a.m. to 8:00 p.m.

Passes/Permits/Fees: The fee to visit the Jordan Schnitzer Museum of Art is $5 for adults and $3 for seniors ages 62 and older. University of Oregon students and children ages 18 and under are free.

Closest City or Town: Eugene

Physical Address:
1430 Johnson Lake
Eugene, OR 97403

GPS Coordinates: 44.04511° N, 123.07718° W

Did You Know? The Jordan Schnitzer Museum of Art is the only academic art museum in the state that is accredited by the American Alliance of Museums.

Valley of the Giants

Located in Northwest Oregon, this incredible forest preserve is home to some of the state's largest Douglas firs and western hemlock trees, many of which approach 500 years in age. An easy 1.4-mile hiking trail leads you to through these giants, and though the elevation gain is less than 690 feet, there are occasional steep sections where you will want to watch your step and be mindful of roots.

Best Time to Visit: The best time to visit the Valley of the Giants is between December and July, as it's closed the rest of the year for fire season.

Passes/Permits/Fees: It is free to visit.

Closest City or Town: Falls City

Physical Address:
Falls City Chamber of Commerce
299 Mill Street
Falls City, OR 97344

GPS Coordinates: 44.9399° N, 123.7137° W

Did You Know? "Big Guy" was one of the valley's most famous trees. Though it was blown down in a windstorm in 1981, the 230-foot-tall tree was thought to be over 600 years old.

Darlingtonia State Natural Site

An 18-acre botanical park, the Darlingtonia State Natural Site is the only park property in the state that's dedicated to protecting a single plant species. The *Darlingtonia californica*, or the cobra lily, is a rare carnivorous plant and the only member of the pitcher plant family to exist in Oregon. This yellowish-green plant stands 10–20 inches high. It features purplish and reddish leaves that protect a hidden opening containing the nectar that attracts the insects that the plant eats. The site includes hiking trails, a picnic area, and flushing restrooms.

Best Time to Visit: The cobra lily blooms in late spring through early summer.

Passes/Permits/Fees: There is no fee to visit.

Closest City or Town: Florence

Physical Address:
5400 Mercer Lake Road
Florence, OR 97439

GPS Coordinates: 44.04633° N, 124.09674° W

Did You Know? The name *cobra lily* comes from its flared tubular leaves that look like the head of a snake and feature a red forked "tongue" (red leaf).

Sea Lion Caves

Located around the midpoint of the Oregon Coast, the Sea Lion Caves are the year-round home of the Steller sea lion (though the California sea lion has been known to make an appearance). An elevator will take you down to the cave where you can see the sea lions themselves. This area is also home to other coastal animals such as sea birds, and you can view migrating gray whales and orcas from the whale-watching deck.

Best Time to Visit: The sea lions come and go as they please, so the wildlife preserve recommends calling ahead for the status of the sea lions.

Passes/Permits/Fees: Admission is $14 for adults, $13 for seniors, $8 for children ages 5 to 12, and free for children under the age of 4. There is no parking fee.

Closest City or Town: Florence

Physical Address:
Sea Lion Caves
91560 US-101
Florence, OR 97439

GPS Coordinates: 44.1218° N, 124.1267° W

Did You Know? Captain William Cox was the first to discover the caves by entering the grotto by boat.

Oregon Vortex

The Oregon Vortex features naturally occurring perceptual and visual phenomena that challenge visitors' beliefs about the laws of physics. In 1904, the "House of Mystery" originally existed as an assay office, but the Oregon Vortex has been documented back to when Native Americans inhabited the area. Horses refused to enter the affected area, and Native Americans referred to the site as "Forbidden Ground."

Best Time to Visit: The Oregon Vortex is open daily from 9:30 a.m. to 3:00 p.m.

Passes/Permits/Fees: The fee to visit the Oregon Vortex is $12.75 per person. Tickets can be purchased at least 3 days in advance on the website, and tours are capped at 20 people.

Closest City or Town: Gold Hill

Physical Address:
4303 Sardine Creek Left Fork Road
Gold Hill, OR 97525

GPS Coordinates: 42.49385° N, 123.08481° W

Did You Know? Until the 1920s, no effort was made to determine the science behind the anomalies in the area.

Trillium Lake

Formed by a dam blocking off the headwaters of Mud Creek, Trillium Lake is a 65-acre recreational lake located southwest of Mount Hood. Locals and visitors come to Trillium Lake for camping, fishing, and photography, specifically due to its spectacular view of Mt. Hood and its clear reflection in the blue waters of the lake. In the winter, it becomes a popular destination for snowshoeing and cross-country skiing. The 2-mile Trillium Lake Loop Trail is a wonderful hike for visitors of all ages and abilities. Swimming in the lake is allowed, and camping is available.

Best Time to Visit: There are activities all year!

Passes/Permits/Fees: There is a $5 fee per vehicle.

Closest City or Town: Government Camp

Physical Address:
Mt. Hood Cultural Center & Museum
88900 Government Camp Loop
Government Camp, OR 97028

GPS Coordinates: 45.27124° N, 121.73895° W

Did You Know? Trillium Lake was originally called Mud Lake, but it was changed because of the millions of Trillium flowers that grow in the area.

Hells Canyon

When European adventurers and homesteaders first stumbled upon the ancestral Nez Perce homeland in the 19th century, they viewed the rattlesnake-infested, sweltering river gorge as a landscape in Hell. To this day, no roads cross the canyon, and many of its points can only be reached on foot. The canyon can be viewed from its plentiful trails or from the Snake River itself on one of the many whitewater-rafting trips offered by private companies.

Best Time to Visit: Visit from late spring to November.

Passes/Permits/Fees: Many activities in Hells Canyon require permits. Detailed, up-to-date information can be accessed on the forest service website.

Closest City or Town: Halfway

Physical Address:
Wallowa-Whitman National Forest
1550 Dewey Avenue
Baker City, OR 97814

GPS Coordinates: 45.5158° N, 116.7567° W

Did You Know? Hells Canyon is North America's deepest river gorge; at 7,993 feet, it is even deeper than the Grand Canyon.

Fort Stevens State Park

Fort Stevens State Park is a military installation that was once used to guard the mouth of the Columbia River for the 84 years between the Civil War and World War II. The 4,300-acre park is a popular place for recreation such as camping, swimming, beachcombing, hiking, wildlife viewing, and exploring the *Peter Iredale* shipwreck. For hiking, there is a 2-mile trail that goes around Coffenbury Lake and 15 miles of other multi-use trails. If you're interested in the park's military history, be sure to visit the military museum, information center.

Best Time to Visit: Visit in the summer when all activities are available.

Passes/Permits/Fees: There is a $5 parking fee.

Closest City or Town: Hammond

Physical Address:
1675 Peter Iredale Road
Hammond, OR 97121

GPS Coordinates: 46.19949° N, 123.97919° W

Did You Know? When the fort was initially constructed in 1863, it was named the Fort at Point Adams. The name was changed in 1865 to honor Isaac Stevens.

Wreck of the Peter Iredale

The *Peter Iredale* was a sailboat that ran ashore on the coast of Oregon on October 25, 1906. It was on its way from Salina Cruz, Mexico to the Columbia River but was abandoned after the wreck about 4 miles south of its destination. The wreckage is still visible, and it is now one of the most popular tourist attractions in the area. It is also one of the most accessible shipwrecks in the Pacific Ocean. The crew of the *Peter Iredale* encountered heavy fog near the Oregon coast and attempted to navigate the ship to the mouth of the Columbia River during rising tide and low visibility.

Best Time to Visit: Visit anytime there is clear weather.

Passes/Permits/Fees: There is a $5 parking fee.

Closest City or Town: Hammond

Physical Address:
Fort Stevens State Park
1675 Peter Iredale Road
Hammond, OR 97121

GPS Coordinates: 46.17914° N, 123.98137° W

Did You Know? The *Peter Iredale* sailboat was named for a well-known businessman in Liverpool, England.

Hart's Cove

This beautiful inlet fed by a narrow waterfall (Chitwood Creek Falls) can be reached after a moderate hike through an old Sitka spruce forest. Some of the trees have been around for 250 years. The area is day-use only, with no overnight parking or camping. The hike crosses two creeks and ends at a prairie meadow where Oregon's wildflowers can be seen for most of the season. Bring something to eat and settle in for a picnic lunch overlooking the beautiful cove while you listen to the seabirds and sea lions.

Best Time to Visit: Hart's Cove is open from July 16 to December 31 and closed the remainder of the year.

Passes/Permits/Fees: There is no fee to visit.

Closest City or Town: Hebo

Physical Address:
Siuslaw National Forest
31525 OR-22
Hebo, OR 97122

GPS Coordinates: 45.0748° N, 124.0012° W

Did You Know? Harbor seals can often be seen in Hart's Cove.

Apple Valley Country Store

The Apple Valley Country Store has been in operation in the Hood River Valley for nearly 30 years. It features homemade small-batch syrups, jams, pepper jellies, pies, pie fillings, and other delectable treats that transport visitors to a time when the area was covered with farmland. If you're not sure what you want to purchase, the country store offers samples of its many jams and jellies. If you just can't decide, you can get an in-store discount when you buy 12 or more jars.

Best Time to Visit: In the summer, there is the Cherry Celebration in July and the Summer Fruit Celebration in August. Join them in September and October for the fall harvests that feature pears and pumpkins.

Passes/Permits/Fees: There is no fee to visit, only to purchase goodies.

Closest City or Town: Hood River

Physical Address:
2363 Tucker Road
Hood River, OR 97031

GPS Coordinates: 45.65464° N, 121.54879° W

Did You Know? The store is a member of the Hood River Fruit Loop, a group that offers 26 fruit stands.

Lost Lake

Lost Lake is located 10 miles northwest of the towering Mt. Hood. The lake sparkles, and the surrounding flora and fauna are colorful and abundant. If you're craving some water fun, the Lost Lake Resort and Campground offers canoeing, kayaking, fishing boats, and paddleboat rentals. If you're more of a landlubber, there are hiking trails ranging from 0.25 miles to 100 miles surrounding the lake, with plenty of opportunities for bird watching, berry picking, and finding waterfalls.

Best Time to Visit: Aim to visit May through June or during the month of September if you're looking to avoid the crowds!

Passes/Permits/Fees: There is a $9 fee per vehicle.

Closest City or Town: Hood River

Physical Address:
Mt. Hood National Forest
16400 Champion Way
Sandy, OR 97055

GPS Coordinates: 45.49560° N, 121.81864° W

Did You Know? The Hood River Native Americans called Lost Lake *E-e-kwahl-a-mat-yam-lshkt*, which means "heart of the mountains."

Tamanawas Falls

Tamanawas Falls flows in a true curtain of water during the right time of year, thundering over a 110-foot lava cliff into a deep pool. Hiking out to the falls is 3.4 miles on an out-and-back trail that follows Cold Spring Creek and is rated moderate. As you pass through the forest, keep your eyes peeled for native plants like fairy slipper orchids and western wood anemone. Tamanawas Falls is also close to several campgrounds in case you want to make a day of it.

Best Time to Visit: The trailhead is open from May to October. This is a good hike for summer due to the density of the forest and the mist from the falls.

Passes/Permits/Fees: There is a $5 parking fee.

Closest City or Town: Hood River

Physical Address:
Mt. Hood National Forest
6790 Highway 35
Parkdale, OR 97049

GPS Coordinates: 45.3972° N, 121.5716° W

Did You Know? Sure-footed climbers can access a dry cave from the trail as well, but it is recommended to bring a rain jacket!

Kam Wah Chung and Company Museum

The Kam Wah Chung and Company Museum is an Oregon state park that seeks to preserve the early Chinese culture that was prevalent during the 1900s. The building was constructed in the 1870s as a trading post and is the best-preserved example of a post–Civil War Chinese mercantile establishment in the West. It was situated along a wagon trail that was later named the Dalles Military Road, and the building was likely a trading post that served mining operations on Canyon Creek. The museum now contains one of the most extensive collections of artifacts from 19th-century Chinese immigrants in the American West.

Best Time to Visit: The best time to visit is between May 1 and October 31, as it closes for the winter.

Passes/Permits/Fees: It is free to visit.

Closest City or Town: John Day

Physical Address:
125 NW Canton Street
John Day, OR 97845

GPS Coordinates: 44.41875° N, 118.95785° W

Did You Know? The Chinese words *Kam Wah Chung* translate to "Golden Chinese Outpost."

Pillars of Rome

These clay cliffs are remnants from Oregon's violent volcanic age that were formed by volcanic ash eroding over time. They stand 100 feet tall, stretch for 5 miles, and are so distinct that they were used as landmarks for settlers braving the Oregon Trail. Bring your camera to snap a few panoramic shots, but be careful when approaching the Pillars of Rome, as slabs of rock could break off and fall with any movement.

Best Time to Visit: The lighting for photographs is best from the late afternoon leading up to sunset.

Passes/Permits/Fees: There is no fee to visit the Pillars of Rome.

Closest City or Town: Jordan Valley

Physical Address:
Jordan Valley Chamber of Commerce
306 Blackaby Street
Jordan Valley, OR 97910

GPS Coordinates: 42.8579° N, 117.6841° W

Did You Know? The rock formations were named by homesteader William F. Stine, who remarked on their resemblance to the ruins of old Roman temples and buildings.

Wallowa Lake Tramway

For a spectacular view of Wallowa Lake and Wallowa Lake Village, take the Wallowa Lake Tramway to the summit of Mt. Howard. At the Wallowa Valley Overlook, you'll see the valley where Chief Joseph, a Nez Perce chief, and his tribe spent their summers. At the Royal Purple Overlook, you'll be treated to a stunning view of the Wallowa Mountains and several of its many high peaks. The tramway opened in 1970 and climbs 3,700 vertical feet to the summit of Mt. Howard, giving passengers a 4,000-foot view of the surrounding area.

Best Time to Visit: Visit during the spring, summer, or fall, as it is closed in the winter.

Passes/Permits/Fees: Single-day passes are $38 for adults and $28 for children ages 4 to 11.

Closest City or Town: Joseph

Physical Address:
59919 Wallowa Lake Highway
Joseph, OR 97846

GPS Coordinates: 45.27684° N, 117.20579° W

Did You Know? The Wallowa Lake Tramway features 25 towers, with the highest at 74 feet.

Baldwin Hotel Museum

The Baldwin Hotel Museum not only serves as the main history museum for Klamath County, but it is also intended to showcase turn-of-the-century architecture in Klamath Falls. Built in 1904, its 40 rooms spread out among 4 stories and are filled with artifacts and antiques that trace Klamath's history from its roots as a timber town to its current position as a major recreation center.

Best Time to Visit: The Baldwin Hotel Museum is open 9:00 a.m. to 4:00 p.m. from Wednesday through Saturday between Memorial Day and Labor Day.

Passes/Permits/Fees: Admission for the 1-hour tour is $5 for adults or $4 for seniors and students. A 2-hour tour is $10 for adults or $9 for seniors and students. Children ages 12 and under are free.

Closest City or Town: Klamath Falls

Physical Address:
1451 Main Street
Klamath Falls, OR 97601

GPS Coordinates: 42.22109° N, 121.78881° W

Did You Know? The Baldwin Hotel was the first building in Klamath Falls to have indoor plumbing.

Mount McLoughlin

Mount McLoughlin is one of the volcanic peaks of the Cascade Range. It's a dormant stratovolcano and major landmark for the Rogue River Valley, with an elevation of 9,493 feet. There is a 5-mile hiking trail to the summit of Mount McLoughlin, which typically requires 6 hours to hike. The trail ascends through rocky terrain and can be difficult to follow but is considered non-technical with a rewarding view at the end.

Best Time to Visit: The trail is open from summer to fall, and snow can appear on the mountain year-round.

Passes/Permits/Fees: It is free to visit.

Closest City or Town: Klamath Falls

Physical Address:
Discover Klamath Visitor and Convention Bureau
205 Riverside Drive
Klamath Falls, OR 97601

GPS Coordinates: 42.4449° N, 122.3153° W

Did You Know? The three Native American tribes that lived at the foot of Mt. McLoughlin—the Klamath, the Shasta, and the Takelma—each had different names for the mountain, which were often important in their stories and traditions.

Old Fort Road Gravity Hill

The gravity hill on Old Fort Road will only take a few minutes, making it a great spot to hit when heading somewhere else. The puzzle of gravity hills—where gravity seems to work in reverse—may be explained by magnetic fields or optical illusions, but watching water run uphill is fascinating, nonetheless. Local legends about the hill vary wildly, with some insisting that the hill is haunted by spirits from the nearby World War II military medical base and others claiming that the road was paved over an old Native American burial ground.

Best Time to Visit: The gravity hill's effect is best seen at nighttime.

Passes/Permits/Fees: There is no fee to visit.

Closest City or Town: Klamath Falls

Physical Address:
Discover Klamath Visitor and Convention Bureau
205 Riverside Drive
Klamath Falls, OR 97601

GPS Coordinates: 42.2517° N, 121.7426° W

Did You Know? The opposite phenomenon of a gravity hill—an uphill path that appears as if it is flat—is called a "false flat."

Neahkahnie Mountain

Climb to the summit of Neahkahnie Mountain and you'll understand why it is named "the place of the god" in Tillamook. Standing at 1,661 feet, it is one of the highest points on the Oregon Coast. The hike to the top requires you to scramble up rocks, but there is a shorter hike that still features some astounding views. Legend tells of buried treasure on the mountain, carried ashore from a Spanish galleon by sailors, one of whom was allegedly stabbed by his comrades and thrown down into the hole on top of the treasure.

Best Time to Visit: In the springtime, the hike offers views of colorful wildflowers.

Passes/Permits/Fees: There is no fee to visit.

Closest City or Town: Manzanita

Physical Address:
Manzanita Visitors Center
31 Laneda Avenue
Manzanita, OR 97130

GPS Coordinates: 45.7440° N, 123.9410° W

Did You Know? Oswald West State Park, where Neahkahnie Mountain is located, is named for the fourteenth governor of Oregon.

Belknap Hot Springs

Featuring two mineral hot spring pools and several gardens, Belknap Hot Springs is a natural wonder that is ideal for relaxation and rejuvenation. The 26-mile-long McKenzie River trail leads from the springs through a fairytale forest. The lower pool is open to the public and does not require reservations. For safety reasons, children must be at least 5 years old to enter the pools. Camping is available and rates vary greatly depending on the chosen accommodations.

Best Time to Visit: Belknap Hot Springs are nice to visit anytime except during winter.

Passes/Permits/Fees: The fee to visit the pools at Belknap Hot Springs is $8 per person for 1 hour or less.

Closest City or Town: McKenzie Bridge

Physical Address:
Willamette National Forest
57600 McKenzie Highway
McKenzie Bridge, OR 97413

GPS Coordinates: 44.19329° N, 122.05059° W

Did You Know? The Belknap Hot Springs are named for R.S. Belknap, who initially found the springs in 1869 and developed the first resort in 1875.

Clear Lake

Clear Lake was formed in a volcanic eruption 3,000 years ago, the lake is so cold that a grove of preserved upright trees that were killed in the eruption is still standing. Take a canoe or kayak out to the middle of the lake, and you can see straight down to the enchanting forest. There are two trails near Clear Lake. The Clear Lake Loop Trail is a flat lap around the lake's perimeter. Rent a canoe or kayak from the local Clear Lake Resort

Best Time to Visit: The water of Clear Lake hovers just above freezing year-round due to its high altitude.

Passes/Permits/Fees: Some trails or day-use sites may require a recreation pass. Current details are located on the forest service's website.

Closest City or Town: McKenzie Bridge

Physical Address:
Willamette National Forest
57600 McKenzie Highway
McKenzie Bridge, OR 97413

GPS Coordinates: 44.3687° N, 121.9944° W

Did You Know? Clear Lake is the headwaters of the McKenzie River, which provides all the drinking water for Eugene, Oregon.

Dee Wright Observatory

The Dee Wright Observatory is a 5,187-foor mountain observatory in the Cascade Range that provides visitors with a panoramic view of 65 square miles of black lava rock. The view is so expansive that on a clear day, visitors are able to see Mount Hood, which is nearly 80 miles away. There are also spectacular views of Mount Washington, Mount Jefferson, and the Three Sisters. Once at the observatory, there is a bronze peak finder that will help you identify your views.

Best Time to Visit: Visit when there is clear weather.

Passes/Permits/Fees: There is a $5 fee per person to visit the Willamette National Forest.

Closest City or Town: McKenzie Bridge

Physical Address:
Willamette National Forest
57600 McKenzie Highway
McKenzie Bridge, OR 97413

GPS Coordinates: 44.26086° N, 121.80145° W

Did You Know? The black lava rock that the Dee Wright Observatory gazes upon closely resembles a moonscape, and in 1964, NASA astronauts conducted drills in the area to prepare to travel to the moon.

Koosah Falls

Koosah means "shining" in Chinook, and this 70-foot drop along the 26-mile-long McKenzie River Trail lives up to its name. The Koosah Falls trail loops out to Sahalie Falls and back, so it's two waterfalls per hike. It's only 2.8 miles total, so this is a great hike for beginning hikers or families with children. Keep an eye out along the trail for viewpoints of the McKenzie River. This is a great area for camping as well, with a few campgrounds just on the edge of the trail.

Best Time to Visit: Trying to get winter access to Koosah Falls can be tricky and downright dangerous. Aim for April through October to avoid any snowfall.

Passes/Permits/Fees: There is no fee to visit the falls.

Closest City or Town: McKenzie Bridge

Physical Address:
Willamette National Forest
57600 McKenzie Highway
McKenzie Bridge, OR 97413

GPS Coordinates: 44.3440° N, 122.0006° W

Did You Know? Sahalie Falls, which connects with Koosah Falls, was featured in the Disney movie *Homeward Bound*.

Tamolitch Blue Pool

Nearly 1,600 years ago, the Belknap Crater released a lava flow that buried a 3-mile stretch of the McKenzie River deep underground. The Tamolitch Blue Pool was created by water flowing up through the underground lava tubes that give the water its unique turquoise hue. A 2-mile hike on a well-maintained trail leads you to look out over the pool. The water is very cold, hovering around 40°F year-round, so swimming is not recommended. The pool is deceptively deep at 30 feet, and several people have died jumping or falling in.

Best Time to Visit: Visit in spring to get the best chance of water runoff being high enough to fall in.

Passes/Permits/Fees: There is no fee.

Closest City or Town: McKenzie Bridge

Physical Address:
Tamolitch Falls
National Forest Road 2672-655
McKenzie, OR 97413

GPS Coordinates: 44.3123° N, 122.0272° W

Did You Know? Tamolitch is a Chinook word that means "bucket."

Evergreen Aviation & Space Museum

This museum dedicated to aviation and space exploration features more than 50 military and civilian aircraft. The Evergreen Aviation & Space Museum opened in 1991 as the vision of Michael King Smith, a retired captain in the U.S. Army and the son of Delford M. Smith, the founder of Evergreen International Aviation.

Best Time to Visit: The Evergreen Aviation & Space Museum is open daily from 10:00 a.m. to 5:00 p.m.

Passes/Permits/Fees: Entrance costs $20 for adults, $15 for veterans and seniors, and $10 for children ages 5 to 16. Children under the age of 5 are free.

Closest City or Town: McMinnville

Physical Address:
500 NE Captain Michael King Smith Way
McMinnville, OR 97128

GPS Coordinates: 45.20479°N, 123.14547° W

Did You Know? The Wings & Waves Waterpark at the Evergreen Aviation & Space Museum is Oregon's largest waterpark.

Table Rock

Just outside of Medford stand two volcanic plateaus, called Oregon's "Islands in the Sky," that are nearly 7 million years old. Upper Table Rock and Lower Table Rock were created by lava flow and then shaped by erosion over time. The tops of the two plateaus feature vernal pools that fill with rainwater. These pools are home to the endangered fairy shrimp. There are two trails to hike up to Table Rock; the path to Upper Table Rock is shorter and slightly easier, though the path to Lower Table Rock is slightly shadier.

Best Time to Visit: Visit during April or May to see over 200 different species of wildflowers in bloom!

Passes/Permits/Fees: There is no fee to visit.

Closest City or Town: Medford

Physical Address:
Travel Medford
101 E. 8th Street
Medford, OR 97501

GPS Coordinates: 42.4513° N, 122.9126° W

Did You Know? Upper Table Rock and Lower Table Rock were once inhabited by the Takelma Native Americans.

Valley of the Rogue River State Park

Located along 3 miles of Rogue River shoreline, the Valley of the Rogue River State Park features both a day-use picnic area and an overnight campground. There's an easy 1.25-mile walking trail along the river's edge that intersects with the Rogue River Greenway Trail, a 4-mile path that winds throughout the park. Its campground features 92 full-hookup sites, as well as tent sites and yurts for rent.

Best Time to Visit: Visit during spring, summer, or fall to avoid trail closures.

Passes/Permits/Fees: There is no cost to visit the park, but there is a fee to stay at the campground. Rates vary based on site selection. See the website for details.

Closest City or Town: Medford

Physical Address:
Travel Medford
101 E. 8th Street
Medford, OR 97501

GPS Coordinates: 42.40991° N, 123.13274° W

Did You Know? Valley of the Rogue River State Park is regarded as a top RV getaway destination in southern Oregon.

Blue Basin

The Blue Basin is located at the John Day Fossil Beds National Monument, which also features Oregon's Painted Hills. The Blue Basin is part of the Sheep Rock unit. The blue color derives from volcanic ash that turned to claystone and then eroded over millions of years. The Island in Time Trail, which is about 1.5 miles round trip, takes you through the basin. The Blue Basin Overlook Trail offers a longer hike with stunning views at just over 3 miles in length.

Best Time to Visit: Since the trails offer very little in terms of shade, aim for a cloudy day or get started in the morning. Bring plenty of water if hiking in the summer!

Passes/Permits/Fees: There is no fee to visit.

Closest City or Town: Mitchell

Physical Address:
John Day Fossil Beds National Monument
32651 OR-19
Kimberly, OR 97848

GPS Coordinates: 44.5912° N, 119.6177° W

Did You Know? While no natural fossil specimens are visible from these trails, the Island in Time Trail winds alongside three replica fossils embedded in stone.

Painted Hills

Oregon's Painted Hills' stripes of red, tan, orange, and black chronicle the shifting climate of prehistoric times. This colorful geological site is part of the John Day Fossil Beds National Monument and was once an ancient floodplain. The multicolored effect originated 35 million years ago as the climate of the area changed over time. The Painted Hills section of the monument offers five hiking trails, fossil beds, and the Visitor Center offers 500 fossil specimens.

Best Time to Visit: The Painted Hills section of the Fossil Beds is open year-round from sunrise to sunset.

Passes/Permits/Fees: There is no fee to visit.

Closest City or Town: Mitchell

Physical Address:
Thomas Condon Paleontology Center
32651 OR-19
Kimberly, OR 97848

GPS Coordinates: 44.6615° N, 120.2731° W

Did You Know? The Painted Hills fossil beds are especially important to vertebrate paleontologists due to the abundant fossils of early horses, rhinoceroses, and even camels.

Mt. Hood

The official title of Oregon's tallest mountain goes to this potentially active stratovolcano that boasts North America's only year-round lift-served skiing. Don't let the term "potentially active" throw you, though! The odds of an eruption in the next 30 years are estimated at 3 to 7 percent, and the mountain is considered dormant. While experienced climbers might want to hike to the top, Mt. Hood offers a variety of other outdoor recreation activities.

Best Time to Visit: Avoid Mt. Hood during summer and spring break to avoid the crowds.

Passes/Permits/Fees: For information about the different kinds of permits needed, visit the state parks website.

Closest City or Town: Mount Hood Village

Physical Address:
Mount Hood Cultural Center & Museum
88900 Government Camp Loop
Government Camp, OR 97028

GPS Coordinates: 45.3736° N, 121.6960° W

Did You Know? Around 10,000 people attempt to climb Mt. Hood every year.

Neskowin Ghost Forest

The stumps that make up the Neskowin Ghost Forest were once Sitka spruce trees, many of which are over 2,000 years old and were once 150–200 feet high. However, the stumps remained buried under the sand of Oregon's Tillamook Coast until 1997 to 1998, when powerful winter storms eroded enough of the coastline to reveal the hidden forest. Today, they are a dramatic and mysterious sight to behold, with 100 stumps crusted in marine life spread out on the beach.

Best Time to Visit: The forest is best viewed at low tide from January through March.

Passes/Permits/Fees: There is no fee to visit.

Closest City or Town: Neskowin

Physical Address:
Chamber Visitor Information Center
35170 Brooten Road, Suite H
Pacific City, OR 97135

GPS Coordinates: 45.1034° N, 123.9809° W

Did You Know? The geologists who studied the Ghost Forest speculate that some natural disaster—likely the earthquake that hit the Cascadia subduction zone in 1700—led to the trees being swiftly buried.

Oregon Coast Aquarium

With the entire Pacific Ocean as its source, the Oregon Coast Aquarium boasts incredible water exhibits. The aquarium's exhibits are known worldwide for their quality, maintenance, and interpretation. While the aquarium is one of the top tourist attractions in the entire state, it's also a vital educational resource, delivering interactive presentations to more than 40,000 students every year.

Best Time to Visit: The Oregon Coast Aquarium is open daily from 10:00 a.m. to 5:00 p.m.

Passes/Permits/Fees: The fee to visit is $24.95 for adults, $19.95 for children ages 13 to 17 or seniors ages 65 and older, and $14.95 for children ages 3 to 12. Children under the age of 3 are free.

Closest City or Town: Newport

Physical Address:
2820 SE Ferry Slip Road
Newport, OR 97365

GPS Coordinates: 44.61832° N, 124.04730° W

Did You Know? A favorite exhibit is *Passages of the Deep*, a 1.32-million-gallon exhibit that provides visitors a 360-degree view of 3,500 sea creatures.

Anthony Lakes Mountain Resort

The Anthony Lakes Mountain Resort is a year-round recreational area that features activities like skiing, mountain biking, camping, summer yurt rentals, and more. Originally opening in 1938, the ski area has been a popular location for locals to view ski races and jumping events and to participate in events like the Winter Carnival.

Best Time to Visit: While Anthony Lakes Mountain Resort is open year-round, the best time to visit is in the winter for the skiing.

Passes/Permits/Fees: A single-day lift ticket for skiing at Anthony Lakes Mountain resort is $45 for adults, $30 for children ages 7 to 12, and $40 for students ages 13 to 18.

Closest City or Town: North Powder

Physical Address:
47500 Anthony Lakes Highway
North Powder, OR 97867

GPS Coordinates: 4.96322° N, 118.23414° W

Did You Know? In 1938, when the Anthony Lakes Ski Area first opened, a daily lift ticket was $0.35 per person.

Salt Creek Falls

Visit one of Oregon's most powerful waterfalls, tucked away in the Cascade Mountains. There is a viewing platform 50 yards away from the parking lot that is wheelchair accessible. If you want a different vantage point, follow the loop gravel trail called Salt Creek Falls Trail or head down a short but steep path to the waterfall's base. Salt Creek Falls is Oregon's second-highest single-drop waterfall, with a cascade of 286 feet, and its pool reaches depths of 66 feet.

Best Time to Visit: The observation site at Salt Creek Falls is typically closed in winter, and the waterfall is the most photogenic in late spring and early summer.

Passes/Permits/Fees: There is a $5 parking fee.

Closest City or Town: Oakridge

Physical Address:
Willamette National Forest
3106 Pierce Parkway
Springfield, OR 97477

GPS Coordinates: 43.6120° N, 122.1284° W

Did You Know? Salt Creek Falls is named for its parent stream, whose downstream springs are often used as mineral licks by wildlife.

Three Capes Scenic Loop

For an up-close view of Cape Kiwanda, Cape Meares, and Cape Lookout, the Three Capes Scenic Loop is the best way to see them all. If you start in Pacific City and head north, you'll come across Cape Kiwanda first. Be sure to look for Haystack Rock, which stands 327 feet tall. Next, you'll come across Cape Lookout, which can only be fully appreciated by hiking the Cape Lookout Trail, a 5-mile out-and-back path. Finally, you'll come to Cape Meares. Be sure to see the Octopus Tree and the 1890s Cape Meares Lighthouse.

Best Time to Visit: The best time to visit is between May and September.

Passes/Permits/Fees: There is no fee.

Closest City or Town: Pacific City

Physical Address:
Pacific City Chamber Visitor Information Center
35170 Brooten Road, Suite H
Pacific City, OR 97135

GPS Coordinates: 45.20161° N, 123.96149° W

Did You Know? At the end of the Three Capes Scenic Loop is Oceanside, a perfect place for enjoying the sunset as it descends on the Three Arches.

Summer Lake Hot Springs

The 145-acre Summer Lake Hot Springs is a remote resort that offers a technology-free escape from daily city living. There is no day-use availability at the hot springs, but there is a campground with full-hookup RV sites and 12 guest houses and cabins. The stunning landscape provides 360-degree views of the scenic area and feature ancient artesian hot water that is known to have healing properties. In fact, the land was originally called Medicine Springs by the Native American tribes that inhabited the area before Europeans arrived.

Best Time to Visit: Summer Lake Hot Springs is open year-round for overnight guests only.

Passes/Permits/Fees: The fee to visit Summer Lake Hot Springs depends on the accommodations and dates you select. See the website for details.

Closest City or Town: Paisley

Physical Address:
41777 Highway 31
Paisley, OR 97636

GPS Coordinates: 42.72802° N, 120.64692° W

Did You Know? The original bathhouse was built in 1929.

Tamastslikt Cultural Institute

The Tamastslikt Cultural Institute celebrates the
Cayuse, Walla Walla, and Umatilla Native American
tribes who have lived in the Oregon area for over
10,000 years. Interactive exhibits and educational
programs take visitors on a 10,000-year journey. This is
the only Oregon Trail museum that tells the story of
western expansionism from the perspective of Native
Americans.

Best Time to Visit: The institute is open Tuesday
through Saturday from 10:00 a.m. to 5:00 p.m.

Passes/Permits/Fees: The fee to visit the Tamastslikt
Cultural Institute is $12 for adults, $20 for seniors ages
55 and older, and $5 for students. Children ages 5 and
under are free.

Closest City or Town: Pendleton

Physical Address:
47106 Wildhorse Boulevard
Pendleton, OR 97801

GPS Coordinates: 45.65434° N, 118.66326° W

Did You Know? The word *tamastslikt* means
"interpreter" since the institute intends to interpret the
tribes' history, present and future, to visitors.

Elowah Falls

This 213-foot drop makes up one of the most beautiful waterfalls in the Columbia River Gorge. The fall is formed as McCord Creek is forced into a narrow channel of water that shoots out over the walls of basalt forming the sides of the amphitheater. The trail is fairly easy and appropriate for most skill levels, with a small amount of climbing and then a summit in the middle of the hike.

Best Time to Visit: Visit Elowah Falls in early spring for the most photogenic waterfall due to heavy seasonal rains.

Passes/Permits/Fees: It is free to visit the falls.

Closest City or Town: Portland

Physical Address:
PDX Welcome Center – Travel Oregon
7000 NE Airport Way
Portland, OR 97218

GPS Coordinates: 45.6119° N, 121.9946° W

Did You Know? Elowah Falls was originally named McCord Falls, but pushback from a mountaineering organization led to the name being changed.

International Rose Test Garden

During World War I, rose enthusiasts were worried that hybrid roses grown in Europe would be destroyed in bombings. In 1915, Jesse A. Currey convinced Portland city officials to establish a rose test garden to provide a safe place for European hybrid roses to grow during this time. By 1918, growers in England began to send roses to the test garden for safe haven. Currey became the first curator of the garden and helped design the facility and its amphitheater. The Royal Rosarian Garden, which was the centerpiece of the original design, contains namesake roses of every Prime Minister of the Royal Rosarians.

Best Time to Visit: Visit between April and October when the roses are in bloom.

Passes/Permits/Fees: There is no fee to visit.

Closest City or Town: Portland

Physical Address:
400 SW Kingston Avenue
Portland, OR 97205

GPS Coordinates: 45.51964° N, 122.70535° W

Did You Know? The International Rose Test Garden boasts 10,000 individual rose bushes.

Latourell Falls

Latourell Falls, one of the multitudes of waterfalls in the Columbia River Gorge in Oregon, still manages to stand out. While most of the area's waterfalls tumble down to some degree, Latourell Falls is a straight 249-foot drop over its basalt cliff. The lower falls can be seen driving by on the Historic Columbia River Highway and visitors can take a short walk to a viewing platform, but there is also a 2.1-mile moderate trail that leads to the waterfall itself.

Best Time to Visit: The best time to visit Latourell Falls is in late spring the waterfall is at its fullest.

Passes/Permits/Fees: There is no fee to visit the falls.

Closest City or Town: Portland

Physical Address:
George W. Joseph State Natural Area
Historic Columbia River Highway
Corbett, OR 97019

GPS Coordinates: 45.5370° N, 122.2178° W

Did You Know? Latourell Falls is part of George W. Joseph State Natural Area, named for the Oregon family who donated the land to the state in the 1930s and '40s.

North Mississippi Avenue

North Mississippi Avenue in Portland is a vibrant shopping district that features live music, independent stores, and acclaimed restaurants and bars. Be sure to stop into Sunlan Lighting, the oldest business still in operation on North Mississippi Avenue. It features lightbulbs of all shapes, colors, and sizes, but there's also an extensive collection of vintage photographs and newspaper clippings that tell the story of Mississippi Avenue history.

Best Time to Visit: Each shop, restaurant, and venue along North Mississippi Avenue has its own operating hours. Check the website for details.

Passes/Permits/Fees: There is no fee to visit North Mississippi Avenue but be sure to bring money to shop.

Closest City or Town: Portland

Physical Address:
Sunlan Lighting
3901 N. Mississippi Avenue
Portland, OR 97227

GPS Coordinates: 45.56175° N, 122.67612° W

Did You Know? Visit the quirky Paxton Gate, where you can learn the basics of insect pinning for display.

Oregon Museum of Science and Industry

As one of the country's leading science museums, the Oregon Museum of Science and Industry was established in 1944 and has become a trusted educational resource for Oregon and beyond. The museum provides exhibitions, public programs, outdoor programs, digital-learning opportunities, traveling exhibitions, and other educational activities to people of all ages to foster a lifelong love of science and learning.

Best Time to Visit: The Oregon Museum of Science and Industry is open daily from 9:30 a.m. to 5:30 p.m.

Passes/Permits/Fees: The cost is $15 for adults, $10.50 for children, and $12 for seniors. Individual exhibits may have an additional fee. See the website for pricing details.

Closest City or Town: Portland

Physical Address:
1945 SE Water Avenue
Portland, OR 97214

GPS Coordinates: 45.50899° N, 122.66584° W

Did You Know? The museum sponsored a fossil expedition in 1951 that was led to the founding of the John Day Fossil Beds National Monument.

Pittock Mansion

The former home of *The Oregonian* newspaper owner Henry Pittock, the Pittock Mansion honors the lives of one of Portland's most influential historical residents. Construction of the mansion began in 1912 and was completed in 1914. There are 23 rooms in the house, including a library and Turkish smoking room.

Best Time to Visit: The Pittock Mansion is open June through Labor Day from 10:00 a.m. to 5:00 p.m. and the rest of the year from 10:00 a.m. to 4:00 p.m. On Tuesdays, the mansion opens at noon.

Passes/Permits/Fees: The fee to visit the Pittock Mansion is $12 for adults, $10 for seniors ages 65 and older, and $8 for children between the ages of 6 and 18. Children under the age of 6 are free.

Closest City or Town: Portland

Physical Address:
3229 NW Pittock Drive
Portland, OR 97210

GPS Coordinates: 45.52580° N, 122.71619° W

Did You Know? Henry Pittock was committed to using local and regional materials to build the Pittock Mansion.

Portland Japanese Garden

Located in Portland's Washington Park, the Portland Japanese Garden features eight distinct garden styles across 12 acres of land. There is also an authentic Japanese Tea House, a stunning view of Mt. Hood, winding walkways, and other natural elements. The garden was conceived in the 1950s when there were growing cultural ties between Oregon and Japan.

Best Time to Visit: The Portland Japanese Garden is open Wednesday through Monday from 10:00 a.m. to 4:30 p.m. The last entry is at 3:30 p.m.

Passes/Permits/Fees: The fee to visit is $18.95 for adults, $16.25 for seniors ages 65 and older, $15.25 for students, and $13.50 for children ages 6 to 17. Children ages 5 and under are free.

Closest City or Town: Portland

Physical Address:
611 SW Kingston Avenue
Portland, OR 97205

GPS Coordinates: 45.51992° N, 122.70688° W

Did You Know? The Kashintei Tea House at the Portland Japanese Garden was built in Japan, shipped in pieces to Oregon, and reassembled in the garden.

Powell's Books

Powell's Books, believed to be the largest independent bookstore in the country, has been serving Portland residents since 1971. However, its roots are actually in Chicago, where Michael Powell opened his first bookstore in 1970. Michael's dad, Walter Powell, spent one summer working in the bookstore with his son and enjoyed it so much that he opened his own used bookstore when he returned to Portland. Eventually, in 1979, Michael joined his dad in Oregon and created a unique bookstore that sold both used and new books.

Best Time to Visit: The Powell's Books flagship location is open daily from 10:00 a.m. to 9:00 p.m.

Passes/Permits/Fees: There is no fee to browse, only to purchase books and gifts.

Closest City or Town: Portland

Physical Address:
Powell's Books Flagship Location
1005 W. Burnside Street
Portland, OR 97209

GPS Coordinates: 45.52363° N, 122.68142° W

Did You Know? Powell's Books is still run and operated by the Powell family—three generations later!

Rimsky-Korsakoffee House

One of Portland's oldest coffeehouses, the Rimsky-Korsakoffee House is located in a 1902 Craftsman-style house that is said to be haunted. This classical music–themed café is named after the Russian composer Nikolai Rimsky-Korsakov and features a casual, community-based atmosphere. Be aware that several of the tables are "haunted" and will elevate, rotate, or vibrate at certain times. For example, the Sergei Rachmaninoff table shakes, and the Stephen Sondheim table disappears through a slit in the wall.

Best Time to Visit: Visit Wednesday through Saturday from 7:00 p.m. to 12:00 a.m.

Passes/Permits/Fees: There is no fee to visit but bring cash to buy coffee as no credit cards are accepted.

Closest City or Town: Portland

Physical Address:
707 SE 12th Avenue
Portland, OR 97214

GPS Coordinates: 45.51840° N, 122.65391° W

Did You Know? There are blank journals placed throughout the house, and visitors are encouraged to fill their pages.

Sauvie Island

The largest island along the Columbia River, the 26,000-acre Sauvie Island is a popular location for kayaking, hunting geese, picking pumpkins, and bicycling. Its flat topography and low-volume roads make it an ideal haven for cyclists. There are three public beaches on Sauvie Island. They're open from dawn to 10:00 p.m. The island is mostly known for its dozens of private fruit and vegetable farms that open for public "u-picking." Hayrides, pumpkin patches, corn mazes, and cow trains are other seasonal popular activities.

Best Time to Visit: The best time to visit is between September and March for harvest and seeing wildlife.

Passes/Permits/Fees: There are only fees for visiting individual farms and picking fruit or vegetables.

Closest City or Town: Portland

Physical Address:
18330 NW Sauvie Island Road
Portland, OR 97231

GPS Coordinates: 45.72066° N, 122.81672° W

Did You Know? Sauvie Island was originally called Wapato or Wappatoo Island by the Multnomah band of the Chinook Native American Tribe.

St. John's Bridge

The only suspension bridge in the Willamette Valley, the 2,067-foot-long St. Johns Bridge spans the Willamette River between the Cathedral Park neighborhood and the Linnton and Northwest Industrial neighborhoods. Before the bridge was built in 1933, the area was served by ferry service that transported 1,000 vehicles per day across the river.

Best Time to Visit: The bridge is wonderful all year.

Passes/Permits/Fees: There is no fee to visit.

Closest City or Town: Portland

Physical Address:
8600 NW Bridge Avenue
Portland, OR 97203

GPS Coordinates: 45.58600° N, 122.76470° W

Did You Know? The construction of St. Johns Bridge began just a month before the Wall Street Crash of 1929, and it allowed many Portland residents to work during the Great Depression.

The Grotto

The Grotto is a peaceful woodland sanctuary located in northeast Portland that's home to more than 62 acres of botanical gardens. In 1924, it was originally constructed as an outdoor Roman Catholic sanctuary that was dedicated to Mary; but today, the grotto welcomes more than 300,000 visitors of all faiths every year.

Best Time to Visit: The best time to visit the grotto is during mass, which is held at 10:00 a.m. and 12:00 p.m. every Sunday.

Passes/Permits/Fees: There is no fee to access the lower-level garden, but admission to visit the upper level is $9.95 for adults, $4.95 for children ages 3 to 11, and $8.95 for seniors ages 65 and older.

Closest City or Town: Portland

Physical Address:
The Grotto
8840 NE Skidmore Street
Portland, OR 97220

GPS Coordinates: 45.55382° N, 122.57366° W

Did You Know? In the center of the cave on the lower level of the grotto is a replica of Michelangelo's statute of Mary cradling Jesus's crucified body.

Washington Park

The 410-acre Washington Park in Portland is one of the state's top tourist destinations, as it is home to the Portland Japanese Garden, the Hoyt Arboretum, the World Forestry Center, the International Rose Test Garden, the Portland Children's Museum, and the Oregon Zoo. It also boasts an archery range, playgrounds, over 15 miles of trails, tennis courts, and several memorials. Washington Park is one of the oldest parks in the city, having been established in 1871 when the city purchased an initial 40 acres of land from developer Amos King.

Best Time to Visit: Visit Washington Park year-round.

Passes/Permits/Fees: There is a fee of $2 per hour to park at Washington Park, and each attraction has a separate entrance fee.

Closest City or Town: Portland

Physical Address:
4033 SW Canyon Road
Portland, OR 97221

GPS Coordinates: 45.51527° N, 122.71019° W

Did You Know? There are 10,000 roses and 2,300 species of trees in Washington Park.

Witch's Castle

Many legends surround the stone ruins of what is known as the Witch's Castle in Portland, Oregon. Tales of murder in the area before the stone structures were built in the 1930s give the Witch's Castle its mystique, but the actual stone buildings were only used as a park ranger station and restrooms for hikers. The structure was significantly damaged in a 1962 storm and subsequently abandoned. The roof caved in, and moss covered the walls. It was forgotten until the 1980s.

Best Time to Visit: The best time to visit the Witch's Castle is any time except Friday nights.

Passes/Permits/Fees: There is no fee to visit.

Closest City or Town: Portland

Physical Address:
Lower Macleay Trail
Portland, OR 97210

GPS Coordinates: 45.52917° N, 122.72494° W

Did You Know? The murder that occurred at this site was that of Mortimer Stump, a man who eloped with his boss's daughter in 1858. Danford Balch murdered Stump for marrying his daughter, and Balch was sentenced to the first legal execution in the state.

Prehistoric Gardens

Since 1955, the Prehistoric Gardens have been a popular roadside attraction along Oregon's Highway 101 Coastal Route. The gardens were the vision of E.V. "Ernie" Nelson, sculptor, entrepreneur, and dinosaur enthusiast who decided to build a dinosaur park. The gardens boast a twenty-minute hiking trail complete with information plaques to educate visitors.

Best Time to Visit: The Prehistoric Gardens are open in the spring and fall from 10:00 a.m. to 5:00 p.m. and in the summer from 9:00 a.m. to 6:00 p.m. The gardens are often closed during winter. It's best to call ahead.

Passes/Permits/Fees: The fee to visit the Prehistoric Gardens is $12 for adults, $10 for seniors ages 60 and older, and $8 for children between the ages of 3 and 12. Children ages 2 and under are free.

Closest City or Town: Port Orford

Physical Address:
36848 US-101
Port Orford, OR 97465

GPS Coordinates: 42.61291° N, 124.39330° W

Did You Know? The 86-foot-long and 46-foot-tall Brachiosaurus took Ernie Nelson 4 years to complete.

Alvord Desert

The Alvord Desert was once a lake that extended over 100 miles, but today it is a cold desert surrounded by three different mountain ranges (the Cascades, the Steens, and the Coast Range). It sees only about 7 inches of rain a year on average. The desert is approximately 12 miles long and 7 miles wide. Camping is free but be cautious. Driving at very high speeds across the flat is a popular recreational activity, and land speed records are attempted from time to time. The desert's geothermal features are also worth seeing, including a few different hot springs.

Best Time to Visit: The ideal time to visit is in the fall.

Passes/Permits/Fees: There is no fee to visit.

Closest City or Town: Princeton

Physical Address:
Malheur National Wildlife Refuge Visitor Center
36391 Sodhouse Lane
Princeton, OR 97721

GPS Coordinates: 42.5354° N, 118.4560° W

Did You Know? The desert is named for General Benjamin Alvord, a Civil War commander who headed up the U.S. Army's Department of Oregon.

Steens Mountain

Steens Mountain is the central peak in the Steens Mountain Wilderness area, which encompasses 170,200 acres. It is located in the high desert and is considered a crown jewel of Oregon's wildlands. Popular activities on Steens Mountain include camping, hiking, picnicking, sightseeing, mountain biking, and exploring the wild and remote land on horseback and foot. Hunting is also available during specific seasons and areas.

Best Time to Visit: The best time to visit Steens Mountain depends on the activity you want to participate in, but summer is the most popular time.

Passes/Permits/Fees: There is no fee to visit.

Closest City or Town: Princeton

Physical Address:
Malheur National Wildlife Refuge Visitor Center
36391 Sodhouse Lane
Princeton, OR 97721

GPS Coordinates: 42.64929° N, 118.57632° W

Did You Know? Steens Mountain's highest peak is 9,738 feet above sea level, and it was originally named the "Snowy Mountains" by fur traders.

Crater Lake

Crater Lake reaches depths of 1,943 feet, making it the deepest lake in the United States. It is also one of the most beautiful, with a vivid blue color that comes from the depth and purity of the water. The lake is the main attraction of Oregon's Crater Lake National Park and partly fills a caldera left by the collapse of the volcano, Mount Mazama, 7,700 years ago. The lake is considered one of the cleanest in the United States; no rivers feed into it, so the lake's water is only replenished by rain and snowfall.

Best Time to Visit: The park is open year-round.

Passes/Permits/Fees: Refer to the forest service website.

Closest City or Town: Prospect

Physical Address:
Steel Visitor Center
1 Sager Building Highway 62
Crater Lake, OR 97604

GPS Coordinates: 42.9446° N, 122.1090° W

Did You Know? One notable aspect of Crater Lake is the famous "Old Man of the Lake," a large tree that has been floating vertically in the water for over a century.

Petersen Rock Garden

The Petersen Rock Garden got its start in 1935 as a pet project of Rasmus Petersen, a Danish immigrant to Central Oregon. He began building castles with moats, bridges, towers, and fountains from rocks, bits of glass, shells, and other found objects. There are gravel trails that wander around the property so that visitors can view the unique rock creations. There also is a gift shop and rock museum on the property, allowing guests to view rare agates, fossils, crystals, geodes, and more.

Best Time to Visit: The Petersen Rock Garden is open daily from 9:00 a.m. to 7:00 p.m.

Passes/Permits/Fees: There is a suggested donation of $6 per person to visit the Petersen Rock Garden.

Closest City or Town: Redmond

Physical Address:
7930 SW 77th Street
Redmond, OR 97756

GPS Coordinates: 44.20405° N, 121.26233° W

Did You Know? The music video for the song "Don't Know Nothing 'Bout Love" by Pennan Brae was filmed at the Petersen Rock Garden.

Owyhee River

The Owyhee River is a tributary of the Snake River, with its headwaters in Nevada but spanning much of southeastern Oregon. This rugged, remote wilderness attracts rafting and kayaking enthusiasts alongside fishers, hunters, and those interested in nature. The Owyhee Canyonlands are home to over 200 species of wildlife. The best way to see the Owyhee is to take a guided tour down the river. The most popular trip is 3–5 days and launches out of Rome, Oregon.

Best Time to Visit: If you're taking a trip or tour down the Owyhee River, aim for April or May.

Passes/Permits/Fees: Registration is mandatory for all boaters prior to launch.

Closest City or Town: Rome

Physical Address:
Ontario Area Chamber of Commerce
251 SW 9th Street
Ontario, OR 97914

GPS Coordinates: 43.8126° N, 117.0254° W

Did You Know? Sacajawea's son Jean Baptiste Charbonneau died after crossing the Owyhee River; his grave is marked off Highway 95 near Danner.

Mount Thielsen Fulgurites

Mount Thielsen, an extinct shield volcano, is known as the "lightning rod of the Cascades," with a pointed top that was worn away over time by glaciers to make the perfect target for lightning during a storm. In fact, Mount Thielsen gets struck by lightning so frequently that the pinnacle of the mountain is covered in fulgurite. These are sculptures that the lightning creates when it strikes; the temperature is so hot that whatever is struck melts and fuses into glass. It's a tough climb to summit Mount Thielsen.

Best Time to Visit: If you're going to attempt to summit Mount Thielsen, aim for late spring or early fall.

Passes/Permits/Fees: There is a $5 parking fee.

Closest City or Town: Roseburg

Physical Address:
Umpqua National Forest
2900 NW Stewart Parkway
Roseburg, OR 97471

GPS Coordinates: 43.1516° N, 122.0664° W

Did You Know? The material that composes the fulgurites is known as lechatelierite, which can only be formed if lightning strikes sand that is nearly pure silica.

Toketee Falls

One of Oregon's most famous falls, Toketee is named for the Chinook word meaning "pretty" or "graceful." It's known for the elegant basalt formation that frames its two-stage, 120-foot drop. The trail out to the falls is less than 1 mile round trip and recommended for all ages. If you want to get a bit closer to the falls, it is easy enough to shimmy through the fencing and work your way down. Wear proper footwear, but the rest of the way down is not too challenging as long as you take your time.

Best Time to Visit: The trail to Toketee Falls is open year round. Parking is tight, so avoid the weekends.

Passes/Permits/Fees: There is no fee to visit.

Closest City or Town: Roseburg

Physical Address:
Umpqua National Forest
2900 NW Stewart Parkway
Roseburg, OR 97471

GPS Coordinates: 43.2633° N, 122.4337° W

Did You Know? Due to its reliable water flow, Toketee Falls actually ignores the fluctuation in flow during the summer that affects many of Oregon's falls.

Umpqua Hot Springs

Among the most popular in the state, Umpqua Hot Springs features several pools located under a forested canopy in southern Oregon. Also known as Toketee Hot Springs, the pools boast a water temperature of up to 115°F—some of the warmest in the state. The hottest pool is located at the top of a steep 0.4-mile hike, and the pools that dot the hillside get cooler the lower they are situated. While you aren't allowed to camp at Umpqua Hot Springs, the Toketee Lake Campground is located within 3 miles of the pools and is open year-round. The pools are only open during the day.

Best Time to Visit: The best time to visit the Umpqua Hot Springs is between April and October.

Passes/Permits/Fees: There is a $5 daily fee per vehicle to visit the Umpqua Hot Springs.

Closest City or Town: Roseburg

Physical Address:
2900 NW Stewart Parkway
Roseburg, OR 97471

GPS Coordinates: 43.29762° N, 122.36570° W

Did You Know? These are clothing-optional hot springs.

Umpqua National Forest

The Umpqua National Forest has three different Wilderness areas: Boulder Creek Wilderness, Mount Thielsen Wilderness, and Rogue Umpqua Divide Wilderness. The Umpqua National Forest offers camping sites, over 300 miles of trails maintained for year-round use, and fishing at Diamond Lake. The Forest has several waterfalls, including the 272-foot Watson Falls. Or enjoy the forest by driving down the Rogue-Umpqua National Scenic Byway for a great view!

Best Time to Visit: The best time to visit Umpqua is during the fall to see the autumn foliage.

Passes/Permits/Fees: Some activities may require a recreation pass. Visit the forest service's website for more details.

Closest City or Town: Roseburg

Physical Address:
Umpqua National Forest
2900 NW Stewart Parkway
Roseburg, OR 97471

GPS Coordinates: 43.2189° N, 122.6193° W

Did You Know? The word *Umpqua* can translate to either "thundering waters" or "across the waters."

Willamette Valley

More than 600 wineries are located in Willamette Valley, which is why it's celebrated as Oregon's wine country. But there's a lot more to see in Willamette Valley than just grapes and wine. It's also known for vibrant arts and culture scene, Oregon truffles, hazelnut farms, covered bridges, breathtaking waterfalls, and numerous museums that commemorate the heritage and history of the region.

Best Time to Visit: The best time to visit Willamette Valley is between Memorial Day and Labor Day, when the vineyards are blooming.

Passes/Permits/Fees: There is no cost to visit Willamette Valley, but individual attractions may have their own fees.

Closest City or Town: Salem

Physical Address:
Willamette Valley Visitors Association
388 State Street, Suite 100
Salem, OR 97301

GPS Coordinates: 45.03898° N, 122.94846° W

Did You Know? The Willamette Valley is home to about 70 percent of Oregon's total population.

Silver Falls

Silver Falls State Park is home to the Trail of Ten Falls, a nationally recognized 7-mile hike that leads you through a dense forest up to ten beautiful waterfalls, ranging from the 27-foot Drake Falls to the remote, 177-foot South Falls. The hike is classified as moderate, so if that's not your thing, check out South Falls from the viewing bridge or visit the Silver Falls Riding Stables for a guided horseback ride.

Best Time to Visit: This park is one of the easier parks to visit in winter since it doesn't get too snowy, but the falls are still full from late March to May.

Passes/Permits/Fees: There is a $5 day-use parking fee to visit Silver Falls.

Closest City or Town: Silverton

Physical Address:
Silver Falls State Park
20024 Silver Falls Highway SE
Sublimity, OR 97385

GPS Coordinates: 44.8652° N, 122.6262° W

Did You Know? Silver Falls State Park was used as a filming location for several blockbuster films, including *The Hunted* and *Twilight*.

Smith Rock

Not many places can claim to be the birthplace of a sport, but the American sport of climbing was born at Smith Rock. Smith Rock itself is a 3,200-foot ridge with a sheer cliff face overlooking the Crooked River. The rock is made out of layers of tuff, formed by volcanic ash from approximately 30 million years ago, as well as more recent layers of basalt from approximately half a million years ago. Even if you're not much of a climber, Smith Rock offers opportunities for hiking and biking.

Best Time to Visit: The park is open year-round from dawn to dusk, but some climbing areas have limited access from about January 15 to August 1.

Passes/Permits/Fees: A $5 day-use permit is required per vehicle.

Closest City or Town: Terrebonne

Physical Address:
Visitor Center at Smith Rock
10260 NE Crooked River Drive
Terrebonne, OR 97760

GPS Coordinates: 44.3682° N, 121.1406° W

Did You Know? This state park has over 1,800 rock climbing routes as of 2010.

Bridgeport Village

A popular shopping destination known as a lifestyle center, Bridgeport Village boasts an open-air street mall that features internationally renowned stores. Once you've shopped, be sure to visit one or more of the 12+ restaurants in the area. You can also turn your visit into a luxury experience by availing yourself of concierge services, which can include spa and restaurant bookings, valet parking, and free use of umbrellas.

Best Time to Visit: Bridgeport Village is open daily from 10:00 a.m. to 8:00 p.m.

Passes/Permits/Fees: There is no fee to visit Bridgeport Village, but since it's a shopping area, be sure to bring some money.

Closest City or Town: Tigard

Physical Address:
7455 SW Bridgeport Road
Tigard, OR 97224

GPS Coordinates: 45.39487° N, 122.75390° W

Did You Know? Bridgeport Village was originally the site of a county-owned rock quarry that ended operations in the 1980s.

Cape Meares

Cape Meares features some of Oregon's most incredible views. In fact, most of the cape is part of the Cape Meares State Scenic Viewpoint, which offers 3 miles of hiking trails up to the top of the bluff. Gaze at the Oregon Coast before heading to Cape Meares Lighthouse and taking a free tour. In addition to the baffling Octopus Tree, Cape Meares is home to the Big Spruce, Oregon's largest Sitka tree at 144 feet.

Best Time to Visit: The best time to visit Cape Meares is between April and July for the chance at spotting migrating gray whales and nesting seabirds in the cliffs and offshore rocks.

Passes/Permits/Fees: There is no fee to visit.

Closest City or Town: Tillamook

Physical Address:
Tillamook Visitors Center
208 Main Avenue
Tillamook, OR 97141

GPS Coordinates: 45.4898° N, 123.9587° W

Did You Know? Cape Meares Lighthouse is the shortest lighthouse on the Oregon Coast at just 38 feet.

The Octopus Tree

This 105-foot tree has also been called the Candelabra Tree, the Monstrosity Tree, and the Council Tree. It has no central trunk; instead, the tree base splits into six limbs that extend out up to 16 feet before shooting upwards, giving the tree the appearance of an inverted octopus. There are several different theories on how the tree came to be shaped. Some suggest it was done by extreme wind, while local historians believe that it was done by Native Americans who shaped the tree for burial purposes. The hike to the tree is less than half a mile through Cape Meares State Park.

Best Time to Visit: Visit during the spring or winter to spot migrating gray whales from the Scenic Viewpoint.

Passes/Permits/Fees: It is free to visit.

Closest City or Town: Tillamook

Physical Address:
Tillamook Visitors Center
208 Main Avenue
Tillamook, OR 97141

GPS Coordinates: 45.48511° N, 123.97258° W

Did You Know? Trees that were shaped by Native Americans are known as culturally modified trees.

Oneonta Gorge

Oneonta Gorge is a slot canyon that features the Oneonta Trail, a route that leads to Lower Oneonta Fall in the Mark O. Hatfield Wilderness. The gorge, which is covered with brilliantly colored lichen, is one of the most picturesque locations in the Columbia River Gorge National Scenic Area. The trail through the gorge is just 0.3 miles long, but it is difficult and can be treacherous in wet conditions. There is a large logjam before you get to the falls, and pools may require chest-high wading if you want to reach the 100-foot Lower Oneonta Falls.

Best Time to Visit: Visit in the spring, summer, or fall during the week to avoid crowds.

Passes/Permits/Fees: There is a $5 fee per vehicle.

Closest City or Town: Troutdale

Physical Address:
West Columbia Gorge Chamber of Commerce
107 E. Historic Columbia River Highway
Troutdale, OR 97060

GPS Coordinates: 45.58009° N, 122.07245° W

Did You Know? The trail through Oneonta Gorge is not an official path and therefore isn't maintained. It is recommended to stop at the logjam.

Enchanted Forest

Enchanted Forest conceived by Roger Tofte in the 1960s as a place for him and his family. What was essentially the Tofte's backyard became filled with storybook characters, small buildings, and "rides." After 7 years of work, Enchanted Forest opened in August 1971. Since then, the Tofte family has continued to add more attractions to Roger's dream.

Best Time to Visit: Enchanted Forest is open weekends in April, May, and September from 10:30 a.m. to 5:00 p.m. and daily in June, July, and August.

Passes/Permits/Fees: The fee to visit Enchanted Forest is $22 per person for visitors ages 13 and older, $19 per person for seniors ages 62 and older, and $19 for children ages 3 to 12. Children ages 2 and under are free to enter but must pay for individual rides.

Closest City or Town: Turner

Physical Address:
8462 Enchanted Way SE
Turner, OR 97392

GPS Coordinates: 44.83201° N, 123.00873° W

Did You Know? Opening day only attracted 75 visitors, but word quickly spread, and the second day saw 1,000.

Cottonwood Canyon State Park

The 8,000-acre Cottonwood Canyon State Park is known for its immense vertical cliffs carved by the John Day River contrasted with rocky grasslands that seem to go on for miles in every direction. The John Day River runs for 252 miles and offers some of the best steelhead fishing in the Pacific Northwest. Visitors can enjoy floating down the river in rafts, canoes, drift boats, and kayaks. Hiking is another popular activity, with both groomed and primitive trails to explore.

Best Time to Visit: Year-round camping is available.

Passes/Permits/Fees: There is no fee to visit unless you decide to camp overnight.

Closest City or Town: Wasco

Physical Address:
The Dalles Lock and Dam Visitors Center
3545 Bret Clodfelter Way
The Dalles, OR 97058

GPS Coordinates: 45.45732° N, 120.41787° W

Did You Know? Cottonwood Canyon State Park is the second largest in Oregon, after Silver Falls State Park.

Wooden Shoe Tulip Farm

Established in 1950 as a family farm, the Iverson family started growing tulips in 1974. By the 1980s, more than 15 acres of land were dedicated to growing tulips, and the family discovered they needed to expand to meet the growing demand for the flowers. Thus, the Wooden Shoe Bulb Company was created in 1983. In 1985, the family opened the fields for Easter weekend for the first time and found its niche in growing and selling tulips. The name was changed to the Wooden Shoe Tulip Farm in 2001, and today, the fields are open for an entire month between the end of March and the first week of May, a period known as the Tulip Festival.

Best Time to Visit: The best time to visit is in April.

Passes/Permits/Fees: Season passes are $60. Daily passes are $15 on weekdays and $20 on weekends.

Closest City or Town: Woodburn

Physical Address:
33814 S. Meridian Road
Woodburn, OR 97071

GPS Coordinates: 45.11925° N, 122.74864° W

Did You Know? The Tulip Festival now encompasses 40 acres of tulips at the Wooden Shoe Tulip Farm.

Devil's Churn

Devil's Churn is an inlet that was carved over thousands of years as waves lashed against the basalt shoreline. This formed an underwater sea cave whose roof eventually collapsed. Now, when the tide comes in, Devil's Churn hurls the water several hundred feet in the air! Visitors are permitted to walk down to the volcanic rock surrounding the churn and can even cross over to the far side. It's important to be extremely cautious, both with the waves and with your footing.

Best Time to Visit: Devil's Churn is open year-round, but in the winter, the waves can be especially strong and deadly. Aim to visit during high tide.

Passes/Permits/Fees: There is a $5 parking fee.

Closest City or Town: Yachats

Physical Address:
Yachats Area Chamber of Commerce
241 Oregon Coast Highway
Yachats, OR 97498

GPS Coordinates: 44.2846° N, 124.1157° W

Did You Know? Devil's Churn is really more of a funnel, but it's easy to see why that name wouldn't have stuck as well.

Thor's Well

Thor's Well is sometimes called "the drainpipe of the Pacific." At first glance, it looks like a seemingly bottomless sinkhole. The well is actually just a large hole in the rock that's likely only about 20 feet deep. Some researchers theorize that the well started out as a sea cave. The roof eventually collapsed and created openings at the top and bottom of the cave, which is what causes the wild spray out of the top of the well. If you venture out to the rocks, use extreme caution. This area can be dangerous; never turn your back on the waves, and be careful with your footing.

Best Time to Visit: Try aiming to arrive one hour before high tide.

Passes/Permits/Fees: There is no fee to visit.

Closest City or Town: Yachats

Physical Address:
Thor's Well (Cape Perpetua Scenic Area)
2311-2399 Oregon Coast Hwy
Florence, OR 97439

GPS Coordinates: 44.2784° N, 124.1135° W

Did You Know? In March through June, migrating gray whales are often spotted along the coastline.

Proper Planning

With this guide, you are well on your way to properly planning a marvelous adventure. When you plan your travels, you should become familiar with the area, save any maps to your phone for access without internet, and bring plenty of water—especially during the summer months. Depending on which adventure you choose, you will also want to bring snacks or even a lunch. For younger children, you should do your research and find destinations that best suit your family's needs. You should also plan when and where to get gas, local lodgings, and food. We've done our best to group these destinations based on nearby towns and cities to help make planning easier.

Dangerous Wildlife

There are several dangerous animals and insects you may encounter while hiking. With a good dose of caution and awareness, you can explore safely. Here are steps you can take to keep yourself and your loved ones safe from dangerous flora and fauna while exploring:

- Keep to the established trails.
- Do not look under rocks, leaves, or sticks.
- Keep hands and feet out of small crawl spaces, bushes, covered areas, or crevices.
- Wear long sleeves and pants to keep arms and legs protected.
- Keep your distance should you encounter any dangerous wildlife or plants.

Limited Cell Service

Do not rely on cell service for navigation or emergencies. Always have a map with you and let someone know where you are and how long you intend to be gone, just in case.

First Aid Information

Always travel with a first aid kit in case of emergencies.

Here are items you should be certain to include in your primary first aid kit:

- Nitrile gloves
- Blister care products
- Band-Aids in multiple sizes and waterproof type
- Ace wrap and athletic tape
- Alcohol wipes and antibiotic ointment
- Irrigation syringe
- Tweezers, nail clippers, trauma shears, safety pins
- Small zip-lock bags containing contaminated trash

It is recommended to also keep a secondary first aid kit, especially when hiking, for more serious injuries or medical emergencies. Items in this should include:

- Blood clotting sponges
- Sterile gauze pads
- Trauma pads
- Second-skin/burn treatment

- Triangular bandages/sling
- Butterfly strips
- Tincture of benzoin
- Medications (ibuprofen, acetaminophen, antihistamine, aspirin, etc.)
- Thermometer
- CPR mask
- Wilderness medicine handbook
- Antivenin

There is much more to explore, but this is a great start.

For information on all national parks, visit https://www.nps.gov/index.htm .

This site will give you information on up-to-date entrance fees and how to purchase a park pass for unlimited access to national and state parks. This site will also introduce you to all of the trails at each park.

Always check before you travel to destinations to make sure there are no closures. Some hiking trails close when there is heavy rain or snow in the area and other parks close parts of their land for the migration of wildlife. Attractions may change their hours or temporarily shut down for various reasons. Check the websites for the most up-to-date information.

Made in the USA
Las Vegas, NV
13 January 2023

65564687R00079